SMILE, YOU ARE UNDER SURVEILLANCE!

THE ULTIMATE HOW-TO LAYMAN'S GUIDE TO CYBERPRIVACY

AS EXPLAINED BY A 16-YEAR-OLD

By Hugo Alejandro Cuenca
Just another 16 year-old kid

Warning and Disclaimer: If you are going to copy the whole book or parts of it, be cool and at least mention its title and my full name. And if you want to make a fast buck, then register with Amazon.com and use their link to my book. That way you make some dinero and I do too. It's a tough world, buddy. In any case, if you don't do it out of laziness or you just plain forgot about it, I will not go after you with the Copyright Police, but man, it's the least you can do for both of us.

All the stuff that I've written here comes from my own experience and by reading a lot, and I mean a lot of related articles. So, if you are going to heed my advice, remember that I am just another 16 year-old kid wanting to help, hence it's your responsibility if you mess something up, so later don't go around blaming me or the publishers or anyone related to this book. And stop whining and grow up, man!

Acknowledgements: To my parents and to my sister for being so patient in this and the rest of my projects.

To my school *Colegio San Ignacio*, for being so supportive, rigorous and challenging, in helping me develop a critical and independent thinking, geared to help those most needed.

To my teachers who gave me all they had to further advance my quest for knowledge and excellence.

To all of my friends, especially all of those in our Class 2018, or known by everyone as *Promoción 91*, for being so supportive in all that I do.

Hugo Alejandro Cuenca

Chapter 1:
Who am I?

With the way technology is moving nowadays, it may not surprise you that I began writing this book when I was 13. Yes, somewhat old for the new standards, you may think, but alas, I also had a school life to attend, some socializing to do... I mean, I have a life too, you know.

Anyhow, this part of my book is for me, believe it or not, the hardest one, because I have to briefly explain who I am, what I do, my favorite color, and stuff like that, and that makes me uncomfortable. I prefer to have some one else, like my grandmother tooting the horn for me. That is grannies' turf.

And talking about oldies, I recall back when I was reeeeally young. Like 4 years ago. I think that moment changed my life forever. I compare it to the aha!-moment that Leonardo Da Vinci had when he realized that he could paint, or the moment when Euler said, yes, I can solve that math problem.

My aha moment happened in a wild, jungle-like place close to home. A place surrounded with all types of feral animals.

It was the moment when I stumbled across a monster, a wild beast. One that you could smell from miles afar. A humongous animal like none you have seen before. A monster, that once awake, howled a horrifying noise that could be heard across from that place.

A beast that could render anyone breathless and scared in less than a second.
A beast covered with hair that resembled colored copper wires, and a shiny fur that was like an armor. I, like my predecessors who had encountered it previously, covered my eyes with my arms, and remained motionless on the spot. I could not move. Panic got a hold of me. I visualized in my mind the beast smelling my fear and getting ready to jump at and devour me.

But suddenly, a surge of power came to me. A need, coming from my innermost, pushing me to fight the beast went through my blood stream straight to my already pumping heart. In spite of my paralyzing fear, I now wanted to fight the monster face to face. A primitive call was pushing me to dominate and conquer it, like no one in my family had done before. But I was alone. No one could help me if I failed. It was going to be me and the beast. Just the two of us. Could I do it?

Once I got a hold of myself, I grabbed the utensil closet to me to defend myself against this wild animal, and maybe, just maybe, dominate it. So, I began to swing my new weapon from hand to hand, trying to distract the beast. And although my weapon was just a screwdriver, it was enough for me to do what had to be done. Seconds became minutes, and minutes seemed like hours in an endless, excruciating fight against the monster.

Finally, I pushed my weapon carefully into the beast's fur, into its shiny armor, trying to reach its innards. And then I began to move that screwdriver skilfully… until I opened the animal up. And there it was, I had defeated the beast. Now it was without its fur and with all its wire-like hairs opened for me to contemplate. I, a 9 years-old boy, alone against the elements, had defeated it!

After opening it, it was my first encounter with the innards of a PC. Definitively a wild monster to me. Now, screwdriver in hand and shouting like Tarzan I had conquered my fear of gizmos and in fact I was savoring my aha moment. After it, I started to understand why that monstrous PC made those terrifying noises, and why it had all those wire sticking up like hairs out of its guts.

I will skip the gory details of how I removed the power supply from this indomitable beats, and how I pulled out the spider-like integrated circuits off of the animal. But I will tell you that after that experience, my life changed. I began to understand how computers worked, and how software was their food.

So, if you happen to be a grown-up reading this, my advise to you is to let your children, little brother/sister/cousin, explore the gadgets you have at home. Make sure to unplug them first, and let them explore. It's a wild world out there.

After my encounter with the beast, I realized that what I liked the most was to make it do things. So I taught myself a very simple to use language: python. With it, I developed a software to measure angles and other neat things. So, what I would do was to apply whatever subject I was learning at school and try to make a software for it. It was fun.

I was doing it while I practiced violin with the school Orchestra. Then, when I helped others as a Math tutor at the school. In the mean time I received the Academic Excellence Award granted by the US President, I became a member of the National Junior Honor Society, the Math Honor Society, the Venezuelan Harvard Model of United Nations, and picked up some medals at the US and Venezuelan Math Olympics.

Then, when I published my first App, the servers where I had hosted my free website advertising it, collapsed and I was kicked out of it for generating too much traffic. That was embarrassing. But when I learned why it had happened it became exhilarating. My first App had been a success.

Most of that was even before I was 13.

But, let's not get ahead of ourselves. Let me tell you a story.

Some people, especially journalists, have asked me how I came up with my first App. Well here is the story.

My grandmother used to have an old cell phone. One so slow and old, that it could be easily compared to a living dinosaur. A specimen that could hardly surf the Internet, and that was ready to be obliterated by the advance of technology.

But I love my grandmother and I wanted to help her without having her obliterate her savings. So, I began a project that could help her old cell phone at least surf the Internet without crashing.

While working at it, I realized that the solution I was working on was an App. And that it could help Grandma and others as well. Then, after tweaking it, it became clear to me that my App could have many applications too. Some of which I never even imagined when I started the project.

Finally, besides helping Grandma surf the Internet at "lighting speed" with her old cell phone, the App had a more coveted use.

If you may remember, during that time the revelations of Edward Snowden became public, and the world knew that we were all been spied on. It was not an isolated event but a massive operation undertaken by many governments and companies alike. So, you could say that I initially got interested in cyber-privacy and security as I learned more about it developing my App.

In my adolescent opinion, I do understand that some governments need to protect democracy and freedom in their own countries, and ultimately the world, because if they don't they could face terrible consequences.

What I don't agree on is when they over extend their power, or when totalitarian regimes use those same powers to oppress their people. And, of course, I don't agree with criminals using their knowledge to perform evil cyber-deeds on you and me. They are just cyberparasites trying to cyber-kill whoever gets on their way. And that is wrong.

In view of all that, I somewhat changed the Apps' initial use to another that could help people surf the Net super fast, at "lighting speed" with dinosaur-old and new cell phones... but privately. Therefore, I named it PrivatBrowse® And that is the App that made the servers collapse when people began downloading it.

Now, I look back at those memories, and I want to leave a legacy for the generations to come. I want others to dream big and to fight for their dreams, even if that means fighting against imaginary beasts. That is why I am studying (hey, I'm still in school and soon, God allowing, I'll be in College) and working hard in other Apps (the next one will blow your mind, believe me). And hence this book.

But a brief note about this book, booklet or guide, as you may want to call it. First, since I wrote it in a long time span, since I was 13 until now, it may digress a little in some passages, so bear with me, because those passage digressions make it the more

Hugo Alejandro Cuenca

interesting, providing you with a wiser outlook (when I was 13 years old), and a more settled demeanor (now, when I am 16 years old).

Also, I want to point out that I write as I talk, and I talk just like any other person my age in the world would. So, if I use he or she to refer to someone or something, specially in Spanish, I am in no way diminishing the opposite. Likewise, if I refer to adults I do so without the intention of hurting any feelings, heck, we are all going there.

Lastly, I did my best to correct most typos, paragraph digressions, faulty sentence structure, etc., so excuse me if you find grammatical errors. But keep them to yourselves, don't tell my language teacher.

Oh, yeah, I almost forgot. I'm still in High School, so if you deem appropriate to heed the advise of a teenager, fine with me. But I am not liable for anything, like adults say: "this is for entertainment purposes only". I warned you. Beware though, of cyberparasites.

Now I am, as mentioned before, currently 16 while I write this. You may think that it's somewhat old for the new standards of tech writing. But well, what can I say, I waited too long and researched too much, to write this book. Because alas, I also have a school life to attend, some socializing to do... I mean, I have a life too, you know.

God bless.

Hugo Alejandro Cuenca

Chapter 2:
What is this all about?

What you are about to read may shock you. It is not for the faint of heart or the easily grossed-out.
You have been warned! Read at you own peril.

Imagine you are happily walking down the street on your way to school, for an important exam, the one that will determine if you get that scholarship or not; or if you are a grown up, you are all dressed up on you way to your office to make that killer presentation that will catapult your career.

Suddenly, those greasy tacos you ate for lunch start doing their thing and you HAVE TO GO. Of course you worry about your exam or your killer presentation. But your mind, your thoughts are focusing on just getting to a place where you can do your thing. It doesn't matter how close or far you are from your school/office, you HAVE TO GO.

You have time, so not to worry about that. The pressing issue is not time, the urgent need is to do your thing. In the proper place. Privately and without someone interrupting or prying on you, specially in those private moments when the tacos you just ate are having an ultimate guacamole fist fight against your poor stomach.

Now, imagine that you reach the proper place and you proceed to do your thing. Unbeknown to you, the place you chose to go, which was publicly marked as such for everyone to know and see, and to attract others in your similar situation, has hidden cameras, recorders, and all sort of gyzmos to see, hear, scrutinize and smell what you came to do. Grosss! And not only that, they have cameras to film everything and then show it to the world in panoramic cinema vision. Disgusting!

They are the CYBERPARASITES! The invasion of the Cyberparasites!

Well, that's invasion of privacy too.
You are not doing anything wrong or illegal. You are just doing your thing. And then, what you do may be used against you.

I think that is a good simile for privacy, which is the topic of this book.

I once saw a documentary, and when the journalist asked people if they felt bad that there were snoopers all over them, including governments, prying on their Internet surfing habits, they usually answered, that they didn't care if they were spied on, because they were not doing anything wrong or illegal.

Well, tell that to the student or the office executive of the example above.

Bottom line, it is the same thing. It is invasion of privacy.

Now, remember that I started this side use of my PrivatBrowse App as a by-product of the real objective of it, which was to have a "lightning speed" web browser that could be used by new as well as obsolete cell phone owners. But, the thing was that the privacy issue caught my eye, and as I mentioned in the previous chapter, it was the time when Edward Snowden had unleashed all that uproar about it.

The more I researched the more I found that there are many snoopers of all sorts trying to, in a way, be present inside the same restroom facility you are going to in the simile above. That is despicable! I mean, having a snooper next to you right at the moment that you are, well you know, at it.

2.1
Who is snooping on you?

So, my research of this disgusting habit (not of going to the bathroom, but the snooping one) took me to the so called "5 eyes" and to a bunch of other snoopers that are doing their best efforts to take a picture and record everything you do at the imaginary restroom of the example.

But, who are they?

On the one hand, there are public snoopers. Those are governments or government agencies, that have good intentions on paper (the fight of terrorism, the finding of extremists and radicals, the capture of criminals, etc.) to protect us, but those intentions become ill when put into real use. But, how so?

You see, machines and softwares are run by us, humans, and we humans tend to digress a bit, like the paragraphs of this book. We are focused, and then we talk about something else. Well, those who run the government agencies will focus on doing their thing (the fight of terrorism, the finding of extremists and radicals, the capture of criminals, etc.) to protect us, but sometimes they may digress too, and start snooping on people who are not threats against us but that maybe they are threats against them (an ex-girlfriend, they guy who insulted them at the gas station...) or the governments they represent (their political opponents, for example). This is even more demoniac if the government agencies specifically order their employees to snoop on others different from the real threats, because now it is not a digression on the part of bored or ranting employees, but it is an order from the head honchos. Creepy, isn't it?

And that is not all. There are also private snoopers, who are out to get you. I mean they will steal your personal information, they will snatch your passwords, they will empty your bank accounts with no remorse, they may be terrorists, they may be extremists, radicals, and criminals. These people will do really evil things.

They all are CYBERPARASITES!

So there you have it. A cat and mouse situation. The cat, the law enforcement authorities trying to get the mouse, that is the bad guys. Not bad so far. But, what if the cat becomes a sort of eat-all rat, who wants to chase the mouse and also wants to chase and eat people too?

Then, we have a problem.

2.2
The government agencies or public snoopers

Within the public snoopers we have the "5 eyes", which is an alliance of five good guys, of five countries, five cats, who decided to work together, way back in the last century (approx. 1940-ish, and remember, no Internet then) united by an multilateral contract known as the UKUSA Agreement. The guidelines of this agreement stated that those five cats would cooperate in signals intelligence, military intelligence and human intelligence.

The five countries are Australia through the ASD (Australian Signals Directorate), New Zealand through the GCSB (Government Communications Security Bureau), Canada through the CSEC (Communication Security Establishment Canada), the United States through the NSA (National Security Agency), and the United Kingdom through the GCHQ (Government Communications Headquarters).

One of Edward Snowden's sin was to reveal that the intelligence work of the five cats had spread to the Internet.

And, what do these 5 eyes do? Well, according to some hush-hush information, which is top secret material, stuff that is out of the reach of adults and children alike, never ever shared by anyone, classified information that neither your nor I are supposed to know, but alas, that you can find in the Internet, the 5 eyes intercept, collect, acquire, analyze and decrypt information in their geographic areas, and they share that information with each other.

Sounds like Orwell's big brother? Well, it is. The difference, in principle is that the information gathering process of the 5 eyes supposedly pertains to "intelligence" and "intelligence" only. At my 16 years, I tend to believe that initially, since the five cats were in the period called the "cold war", and the moral and ethical values were higher then, they really collected and shared "intelligence" data. You know, the one about preventing other major wars, nuclear bombings, etc. And that was, in my humble and underage opinion, fine.

Now, after time passed, those international tensions relaxed, those country-to-country stresses diminished, and those moral and ethical standards deteriorated, while simultaneously terrorism, radicalism, extremism, and criminality went up the roof. Therefore, I think that initial intention of "intelligence" gathering now tried to encompass also the new threats like terrorism, but for the reasons listed above, it became somewhat lax. Just a little bit. And then a little bit more, and then more. And the word "intelligence" became associated with "gathering everything". And boom!, there you have it, five otherwise cute cats, became 5 snooping eyes (or should I say 10 snooping eyes, because in my understanding countries are not cyclops).

But, with technology so readily available worldwide, not only the five pretty cats are snooping, also smaller countries, dictatorships, and criminal regimes are using the same know-how to snoop on their citizens to persecute and jail them, in order to maintain their autocratic power. Here the cats from a different litter than the other five pretty ones, became people-eating rats. Disgusting and sad!

To recap. Government and public agencies are snooping on you. Period. It is even worse if you live in a dictatorial regime or a repressive state.

2.3
The private snoopers

Now, besides public agencies and governments, and dictators, there are also private people and groups snooping on you. Specially if you are head of state, a president, a rock star, a bank owner, a CEO, a film star, a famous athlete, or anyone with sensitive information.

I know, you may say "I'm none of those, so I'm home free, and no one will snoop on me". Wrong. You may be a target too. It doesn't really matter who you are. The moment you browse the Internet, that you send an email, that you post something on Twitter, Instagram, WhatsApp or Facebook, you are game to be snooped on. If you are, well, just you, **YOU** are a target.

Because, yes, there are criminals (and I emphasize the word criminals, or as I call them, cyberparasites) out there snooping to snatch your passwords, to kidnap the information in your hard disk drive, to obliterate your computer data, to infest you with all type of viruses, to get your personal information and photos and post them anonymously on the Internet, to plan terrorist attacks, and the list goes on.

But besides those criminals, there are also innocent looking companies that like to gather information about you, about your habits, about your linkings, about your interests. They either use your information (data) to push their products or services on you or others, or they sell your information to other for them to push their products and services on you or others. They call it e-marketing, e-technology for the use of commerce, but my belief is that it is nothing more than glorified good'ole marketing.

2.4
Let's summarize it for you

To recap this part, criminals and corporations will snoop on you if they can or if you let them. They are Cyberparasites. If you don't do something, they will devour your privacy and put at risk your cybersecurity. And, if you let them, knowingly or not, they will cyberkill you.

So, in theory, the five cats have a real job, if they restricted themselves to the strict "intelligence" word in the old meaning of it, you know, chasing the bad guys, the mouse, the terrorists. However, since according to my approximation the purpose of the 5 cyclopean eyes has become somewhat lax, or has broadened in scope to include more than "intelligence", then we have an issue, and Edward Snowden saw it, and made it public.

There you have it. Be them public or private, someone is out there trying to snoop on you.
I think that I have provided you with a clear scenario of what is happening in the virtual world. And in a way, it is like the real world, but more sophisticated.

If I continue with the public restroom simile, I could say that, of course there are people that may go to a restroom to write graffiti, or to "casually" drop a piece of Sodium in the toilet to violently make it blow into pieces. Sure, but there are others, like the student or the office executive of the same example, which may be a majority, who only HAVE TO GO to do their thing. And that's it, nothing more and nothing less. And, I don't think that this majority would, nor would you, like to have the world look at you, hear, scrutinize or smell what you do. Much less sell your personal data (noises and photos included) for other to see or to try to sell you something.

In any case, this book is dedicated to you, the good guy. So, I would greatly encourage you if you had alternate plans of doing evil things, to close this book at once and turn yourself in to the next police station. You are the kind of person who has made peaceful Oslo un-walkable, lovely Paris un-livable, and feisty Barcelona scary. You have made the Internet a creepy place by stealing information from users, by cheating on everybody that crosses your path, by terrorizing the world, I mean, shame on you, cyberparasite.

So, again, the intention of this book, is to provide you, the good guy, with an understanding of what is going on out there, and how you may counter it, without obliterating your bank account.

Hey, if I did it for my Grandma, I can do it for you.

Chapter 3:
Why bother with privacy?

What is privacy, and what is all the fuzz about? Isn't our stuff already private? Aren't our conversations private?

3.1
Why bother with privacy?

Well, why not?

I admit that the example of the previous chapter was extreme, and I used to it to relate to you, who may not be technologically savvy, an activity that we all perform on a daily basis, tacos or not, with the concept of privacy.

Since I am sure that you understood the over spiced tacos simile, I could use some more examples related to other mundane activities that you, and we all, do on a daily basis.

Imagine now, after winning the battle against the tacos, that you finished that exam at school and you got an A, so you nailed the scholarship, or that you did your killer presentation at the office and got that career bust, and now you come home to relax, and stay away from tacos for a while. Minutes before, your cable provider had come to exchange the old DVR for a "new and improved" one, at no cost to you.

Great!, you say.

But what if your cable provider, decided to install a mini-camera in your DVR, to see how many in your family were comfortably seating in the couch watching "Game of Thrones" or old "Friends" re-runs? Or checking to see what kind of people you invited over to your house? Or how many more times you HAD TO GO because of the stomach chaos produced by the tacos?

I don't think you would like that.

What if it was not your TV provider but a corporation or a marketing company wanting to start using the mini-camera in your DVR to know if you were eating pop-corn or having dinner while you watch a Batman movie at home? And they would make close ups to see what kind of food you were eating, and discovering that you were not actually eating tacos as you regularly did? Or detecting what type of underwear you were comfortable with while you watched a movie.

I don't think you would like that either.

Even if you play a video game, they could observe your habits. How many hours you spend playing, with whom, against whom, what type of game, what brand of clothes you were wearing, what type of food you were eating. I mean, the possibilities of scrutinizing you are endless.

Imagine if they had a giant check list about you, just by observing your old self seating in the couch with your fav video game. The list would say:

* Playing your favorite game: check mark all days of the week
* Playing while wearing a run down t-shirt: check mark, only in afternoon weekdays, all weekends
* Finger in nose: double check mark, when bored
* Eating chocolate: triple check mark, mornings, afternoons, and evenings
* Scratching your butt: double check mark, one for each side
* Doing your homework as soon as you get home: no check mark
* Having friends over: check mark on weekends
* Snoozing over your term paper the night before it's due: check mark, that very same day
* ...

And after all that snooping, then you start getting advertising in your email, social network accounts such as Facebook, Instagram, etc., you mail box, pushing you and selling you new video games catered to your apparent likings, selling you brand new t-shirts to replace your run down one, selling you exotic foreign chocolate bars, and automatic butt scratchers.

And I don't think you would like to be scrutinized that deeply.

What if you were spied on through your cell phone GPS, and they tracked you right to the same place where you HAD TO GO? What if they could turn your cell phone camera, as well as its microphone, on or off at their will, without you knowing it, and they made close ups to see what brand of paper you were using, or if you read a book while you were at it, and then recorded all the noises you generated in there?

I think you would feel uncomfortable about that, to say the least.

What if they had prying eyes on you while you were surfing the Internet at your home PC, and "casually" they snooped (listen to this, grown ups) your bank accounts?

I don't think any adult would like that.

Well, all that would be considered invasion of privacy. You were not doing anything wrong or illegal, but even so, I don't think that you would have liked to have been observed that close.

Of course there are loonies and extremists out there. And they deserve to be singled out and caught before they do anything wrong or illegal that would harm the rest of the population, including us.
They are the ones that need to be snooped on or scrutinized. Now, to have all the population spied on because of them, that is overextending the issue, and the new real reasons for spying everybody may be different from the original ones, that were to catch the bad guys. And since human beings are those doing the snooping, that same bulk of information obtained from you, if misused, may harm you and the same population that they are trying to protect.

Bottom line: we have to protect ourselves from the bad guys, and from the "good" guys that are trying to protect us from the bad guys. The key word here is WE. It is our work, our duty, we owe it to ourselves to be protected. And no one better than us to protect us. See where I'm going?

Good.

3.2.
What kind of things should you try to protect?

Well, my book will be about the intangible assets that you need to protect. Not the physical ones, like your home, your car, your PC, that you have to protect by using home or car insurance, padlocks, chains, or stuff like that. I will focus on information.

Now, you may ask, what is information? Well, information is all that stuff that is not physical, but that could be used to run physical things. For instance (listen up, adults) your bank passwords, your bank statements, your emails, your portfolios. They are all digital, intangible, but could be used to move you around, they help you do your shopping, to pay your employees, to pay your children their much needed allowances (hint, hint), to take the family on vacation trips to fun places, etc. Other examples could be (listen up colleagues, you underage guys, the minors), our Facebook page, our Instagram photos, our Twitter account, and things of that nature.

In view of all the preceding, we can easily say, that we have a physical life (hey, it's your beautiful self) and physical assets (a home, a car, clothes, a video console, and so on), and a digital or virtual life (who you are and what you do on-line). If we protect our physical life and assets, and our parents generally do, then it makes sense to protect our digital life and virtual assets as well.

I am going to focus on that virtual information that you (and others, friends and otherwise) may have about yourself in the spooky on-line world. A warning, though. What I am about to reveal to you will never be enough to protect you against all evils. The privacy topic is a never ending race, because once you think you have protected yourself, then comes along a new form of snooping you that you didn't know about, and then you conquer it, and then comes another form of attack, and then… and then… and then… You see? Never ending.

Ok, what is this digital or virtual life and assets? That is, simply put, information. Information about you and your assets. D-A-T-A.

In order for you to begin your much sought protection, you first have to decide what kind of digital information you want to protect. What kind of data. Let me give you an example, so you may grasp my idea.

Let's say that you are an inventor. One night you come up with the greatest idea of your life, the next-big-thing. The gadget that the world has been waiting for. The device that investors the world over will beat a path to your door, just to have a glimpse of it. So, the following morning you lay out the diagrams of your great invention in the kitchen table, and turn the TV to watch the news, while you mentally count the many dollars you are going to receive for being such a great inventor.
<u>Potential threats against your privacy</u>: if your DVR had a mini-camera from your cable provider or from any marketing company, your invention would be at risk. Also, if certain government agencies decided to turn on your cell phone camera, your whole project would also be in danger.

Then, all excited, you call Larry the lawyer, your high school buddy, who might help you patent your invention. Larry is currently at an Intellectual Rights convention, talking to a potential client who's asking some questions and who just overheard you shouting over the phone about your invention of the next-big-thing. Larry politely asks you to email him the diagrams and asks you for some advance money to start his work. So, you go to your PC shoot him an email from your personal account, attaching all your diagrams and drawings, and then transfer some funds via your credit card from your company account to his account.

Potential threats against your privacy: your computer could be infected with information snatching viruses reading your passwords and getting all your emails, hence your email could be compromised too and you could also be sending your secret files with your schematics to a different receiver. If your passwords were stolen then your bank and credit card accounts would also be compromised as well as the funds in them. Also, if a thieve breaks into your home you may lose your PC and cell phone, and all the information that goes with them.

After the convention Larry rushes to the hotel's computer center to check on his emails. He is tired so, since there aren't many people in the computer room, he leaves the PC open, and he fetches a soda from a nearby vending machine and then continues with his business.

Potential threats against your privacy: Larry is exposing sensitive information to others in the computer room who could sneak in and check otherwise personal information about Larry or his clients. A stranger could steal Larry's information and even impersonate him and send emails as if it was him, just by looking at the computer (with his email open) and messing around with the keyboard. The attacker could reset most of your passwords from other accounts like (listen up, guys) your Instagram and your Twitter accounts, effectively hacking them and preventing you from accessing them. An even more skilled evil stranger could have planted a virus in that PC to snatch information from users like Larry. If Larry is using a USB device, it could get lost or stolen with vital information in it.

In the morning, once rested, Larry opens up his laptop and starts checking his emails to do some catch-up work, that he could not finish due to the convention. Since Larry is hungry, this time for breakfast, he leaves his laptop somewhat hidden in the closet, and tuns downstairs to grab a bite before he heads to the airport.
  Potential threats against your privacy: By leaving his computer in the hotel room, Larry could be subject to an "evil-maid attack"[1]. All his laptop files could be compromised, as well as the diagrams you sent him with your invention, his personal and business information, etc. If there are thieves around, Larry could lose his laptop and his cell phone with all the information that is within them.

Thankfully, the maids have done the room, so he is ready to finish the work he left unattended before breakfast. Then he goes to the airport, finds a wifi spot, plugs the ac power to his laptop and continues his busy life of sending and receiving emails, updating his law firm's web page, checking if the purchases his company made will arrive on time, renewing his video-movies subscriptions, verifying if you sent him the advance funds, etc. Larry then get the munchies, and runs to the airport snack bar to grab something to eat.
Potential threats against your privacy: Larry's cell phone usage through public wifi networks could compromise his digital security. Accessing delicate business and personal accounts via public spots may jeopardize his and your privacy. Also, thieves could steal his charging cell phone or laptop left momentarily to grab a sandwich at the airport snack bar, with all the information that Larry has in them.

---

1   An evil maid is not a maid that is out to get you.

Enough?

From this brief tale of you and someone doing some business activities you can deduct what are the things that you need to protect. After realizing some of the potential threats faced in each case you could say that they are mainly:

a) your physical devices (smart phone, laptop, desktop, scanner, and any other electronic/digital device)

b) your personal information (passwords, would-be-patents, inventions, ideas, bank accounts)

c) your reputation, your image (who you are and how people perceive you)

But you don't have to be a businessman or a professional person. You could just be a student or a regular Joe chatting with friends, or responding to a message at any of your social networks.
Yes, like I told you before, you could easily be a target for having electronic devices, for having any personal information, and for just being you.

However, those three things above, you should always protect (your physical devices, your personal data, and your reputation). As far as this book is concerned, I will delve into the last two, your intangible assets. It is your responsibility to take good care and protect your physical assets, like your cell phone, your laptop, your desktop, your tablet, or any other electronic device that you may use. So, go get some padlocks and stuff for them.

For protecting you data, this book will introduce you to the world of data protection, that is whatever information is inside and stored in your electronic devices.

So, on to the next chapter.

Chapter 4:
What electronic devices that you own are prone to attacks by cyberparasites?

Another warning. This chapter if very geeky. It may bore you to certain death. Seriously.

But I have written it in such a way that you may survive the geek ordeal and learn some things along the way. For your own good, I would take a deep breath and read it calmly, trying to understand every bit of it, because your security depends on understanding the terminology and the few technical applications described here in every day language.

Please, bear with me. I will guide you by the hand in this tortuous path, but I promise you if you stay by my side, that at the end, you will come out the wiser, and you will even be able to talk some geek. And maybe use a couple of words you learned in this chapter to impress your friends at a party or in your computer class. C'mon, let's go ahead.

First things first. Some vocabulary words to make the most of this chapter. You will notice that I wrote those words in "bold", so you may recognize them.

"**Electronic device**" is any piece or component that controls electricity or rather, the flow of electricity, for instance a diode. Since electronic devices are veeeery small they can be grouped together into integrated circuits. Some times, when an equipment that has many integrated circuits, is lightweight, portable in use, it is electrically powered (it uses a battery or an AC adapter), and it is used for communications, information processing, data storage, or electronic related uses, it is also called an electronic device or a consumer electronic device. Same thing.

The electronic devices that are most likely to be attacked (and also stolen) are:

a) cell phones

b) PCs in all their forms (laptops, tablets, desktops, etc.)

When I say "**attack**" it means that a malicious program may get into said devices and secretly obtain information from you, without your knowledge. The how-do-they-get-into-my-device part we will review later. Right now it's important that you understand the basics.

But, who could dare do such mischievous deeds of getting into your devices?

4.1
Who dares to touch my stuff?

Well, you have two main groups dying to touch your stuff:

a) the bad guys

b) the good guys, which are really bad guys dressed up like good guys

I will delve more on that later in this book.

So, besides the physical attacks (robberies and the likes) on your electronic devices, there are also attacks on what's inside them, and that is, on one hand, your personal information (passwords, would-be-patents, inventions, ideas, bank accounts), and on the other, your reputation, your image (who you are and how people perceive you, photographs, your history, etc.).

But, in order for an attacker to perform his evil deeds on the innards of your electronic devices, he must find first their weakest spots, or what is also known as their "vulnerabilities".

"Vulnerability" is, in short, the inability of an electronic device or its software to withstand hostile attacks coming from the bad guys.

For instance, you download an email that contains a virus, and your PC becomes contaminated. The vulnerability here is the fact that you don't have a virus-scanning software that could detect the presence of a virus that could potentially damage your PC. Same thing for you cell phone.

Other example could be Larry the lawyer, who left his laptop unattended to grab a bite to eat. He left it at the mercy of anyone (a bad guy) who could read the contract he was drafting, or worse copy all of his information to an external device, leaving Larry's work files exposed to strangers or evil doers.
The "vulnerability" here is related not to a piece of hardware or software, but to Larry's carelessness.

Now, I must point out something. Some times, the same software programs that you trust and use daily have hidden and not widely known flaws, also called **"bugs"**, or using your recently acquired language, vulnerabilities. Those flaws or vulnerabilities can be taken advantage of by mischievous minds to install **"exploits"** in your devices. An "exploit" is a malicious software, a chunk of computer code, or commands that will very likely wreck havoc in your device by providing unauthorized data access by the unaware-you to strangers.

4.2
Sophisticated cyberparasite attacks

These unauthorized accesses in general are called "attacks", like mentioned before.

To get a little more sophisticated, and to give you a social tool to intelligently shine in your next party (or cocktail party if you're an adult), you should know that there are many types of exploits. But. Most geeks classify them as:

1)**local exploits**, which mean little bits of computer code (i.e. software) that attack your system allowing a stranger to access and use your device as if he was you. This exploit requires that the evil guy has prior access (physical, like the cyberparasite having your device in his hand; as well as non-physical, like sending you an email with a virus) to your vulnerable device.

2) **remote exploits**, which are those commands (i.e software) that attack the vulnerability of a network, without prior access to your vulnerable system. That means, without you even realizing what happened.

Mind you, more geeky guys classify exploits not by where they are coming from, but by the result of them running the exploits, the so called "attacks". So, to show off at your party, you may also say something like:

"I read about the DoS attack performed last week on so and so company, and I would like to hear your opinion", or " Did you hear about the spoofing attack they pulled on ...". Hey, you can't complain, I'm even preparing you socially here to act like an expert.

Some exploits, but not all, because there are too many, are rather classified by their end result:

1) **EoP, or Escalation of Privilege**, is an exploit (a software) that allows strangers to access resources in your device that are usually protected from other users or from other applications. Having this exploit, the stranger can perform unauthorized actions "on your behalf" or without your recognized permission.

2) **DoS or Denial of Service attack**, is an exploit, commonly known also as DoS attack, where the stranger strives to gain control of your device not allowing you, temporarily or indefinitely, to gain access to it. It's like someone locking you out from your own home, preventing you from entering.

3) **Spoofing**, is an exploit that resembles the mimicry of chameleons, in which a stranger uses a disguise to fool you into giving him access to your system, pretending to be someone else.

4) **Island hopping**, is an attack that uses an already compromised system to attack other systems on the same network

Sometimes, the exploits are made known to the software companies that are affected. So, these companies create what is called a "**patch**", or fix up, and then the vulnerability is rendered useless, because it was revealed and fixed.

Most technically savvy strangers, including governments, and government agencies, prefer not to reveal their exploits, or the vulnerabilities of the affected software, so they can continue using them to practice their dirty jobs.

Some exploits are not known by anyone, and they have not been revealed to the specialized or general public that would immediately create a "patch" to solve the issue. They are only known to those who have found the vulnerability and developed a code to perform an attack. Those are called "zero day exploits".

That means that the vulnerability has not been patched and that strangers may attack the system or the network like there was no tomorrow.

I should also mention that there are other computer assaults or attacks, like the man-in-the-middle-attack, but they don't necessarily involve exploits, or computer codes, they rather make full exercise of the malice of evil doers to get into your telephones, communications, systems, and so forth.

4.3
The Hackers

So far, I have loosely used the word "stranger" to signify someone who is not you, performing the evil deeds. In computerese (the language spoken by geeks) and in popular culture, that stranger is better known as a "**hacker**". However, the term "hacker" is broader than that. Because a "hacker" is anyone who is skilled in programming and who is capable of solving computer problems. Albeit, hackers are better known for breaking into computers that have secure systems.

Another breed of those characters that live in the computer underground are called "**security hackers**" aka "**crackers**", and their only objective is to open up systems via their skilled computer abilities and attack their vulnerabilities. Some are blatant criminals or "**black hats**", and some are just computer security experts or "**white hats**", trying to solve problems originated by vulnerabilities and exploits. However, the general culture sees any hacker as a "black hat" hacker.

Just a tip of information on this subculture: there is a rainbow of "hats" in the hacker communities. Besides black and white, there also are gray hat, blue hat, and ranks among them, like elite, newbie, script kiddies, hacktivists, etc.

Well, now that you know about the types of attacks that your devices may receive, it is worth getting to know a little more about your vulnerabilities and how to counter them.

4.4
Other vulnerabilities

At the onset, I told you that:

"The electronic devices that are most likely to be attacked (and also stolen) are:

a) cell phones

b) PCs in all their forms (laptops, tablets, desktops, etc.)"

Well, those electronic devices, as well as some of your current behaviors make you vulnerable. That is, prone to be attacked by all those governments, government agencies, corporations, guys, hackers, that may have an interest in you. Even if you are a simple Joe.

Same thing as when you leave your laptop unattended, happens when you use super easy and predictable passwords for your on-line accounts, be them banks, credit cards, Facebook page, Twitter, etc. Passwords like "123", "your name", or similar ones, that could be easily guessed by people in the wrong side of the law are prime targets to be used to break into your on-line life. The vulnerability here lies in your naiveté, and not in the device or the software that runs it.

For that reason, I have created the following summarized abstraction of where are the most common vulnerabilities that you may face, and how you can attack them back to avoid being a victim of the bad guys.

There are two main groups of vulnerabilities:

1) **Outside** of your electronic devices

2) **Inside** your electronic devices

I am going to go over each one in detail, with easy to understand advises you should do to prevent attacks.

But before I continue, I must point out something very clearly. The same way that I told the bad guys to stop reading this book in the previous chapter.

If you are one of the good guys, my advise to you is the following. If you don't want anyone to know that you are pondering into joining the bad guys, don't be one or don't do anything to become one. Just don't do it. So, that way you will not have anything to hide, and no one will find anything bad about you, because you actually never did it.

If you don't want anyone to know it, don't do it.

Period.

Now, with regards to the good guys who are not contemplating or even daring to think of becoming part of the bad gang, I have a word of caution.

Even if you are a nice person, you are constantly sending apparently innocuous information through your electronic devices. What is known as unclassified information, the stuff that you don't care if others see. For instance, the photo that someone took of you with that tacky shirt and a clown nose. Or the seemingly inane comment in the email you sent last week. Or the bland statement you posted in your Twitter account regarding the disappearing mountain owl. Or the racial joke you posted in your Facebook page. You know what I mean.

It all seems unimportant, as if you were talking without any purpose, at the end they are just your comments in the ether. No, no, no. They are not and they will not be words blown by the wind. They are there (in the ether) and if not managed correctly they may haunt you forever.

4.5
Opsec

To solve that issue I had to study it a lot more. In fact, I came to know that this whole issue of information use or misuse is a course of study in the military intelligence area. They call it **"Opsec"** (short for Operations Security). And you know, the military tend to be thorough and serious about their job.

In short, Opsec is a process that you have to follow to identify your critical information.

I will give you a short list of what you should know about Opsec, before we go into our thing of protecting your vulnerabilities. Why is that? Because, you have to understand that if you want to protect yourself from the prying eyes of good and bad guys, you need to take certain steps. You have to follow a process. And Opsec is like the way that you must see your information and the world around you from now on.

Once you internalize that Opsec is the way to go, then you can begin to minimize the attacks against your privacy. I see Opsec, like cleaning your home and maintaining it that way.

So, here it is, Opsec in brief.

All the information you generate must pass through certain filters that you must have in place:

1) **First filter: watch your mouth**, you must identify the information that is critical to you. For example, if you are a public figure or a politician, you know that anything you say or do may

eventually be used against you. If you are a person looking for a job, all things related to that position or your past personal information may be of interest for your potential employers. If you are a student, the same thing. So this first filter is related to you. You must assess the type of information you are currently generating, and then make a decision of what you actually want to show to the world. Is that comment you made about someone, appropriate? Could it be used against you if you were running for office, or if you were looking for a promotion?
Think wisely.

2) **Second filter: control your environment**, you must analyze what your real threats are. I mean, if you are an inventor like the example of the previous chapter, you know that there are many people looking to copycat others, including you, so your comments, information, partners, etc. may be potential threats. If you are a businessman, then your competition is a potential threat. If you are a plaintiff in a trial then the defense is a potential threat. If you are at the beach and leave your cell phone in plain sight for others to see, then all people that get close to it may be potential threats. In other words, you can control your situations so as not to become paranoid and see all others around you as potential threats. You just have to analyze each situation and work from there.

3) **Third filter: know your weakness**, here you have to analyze your vulnerabilities. You have to approach your regular behavior, your day to day routine, and analyze it. I mean, do you use a cell phone, do you have a laptop, do you have passwords, are your passwords easy to figure out, do you share your home computer with your buddies, do you use an external pen drive while you work at a cybercafe? For instance, you wake up to the sound of your cell phone that you use as an alarm clock, then you use the same cell phone to read the news. At the same time you turn your

laptop on while your shower warms up. With all that raucous you're making your sister wakes up and turns your PC on to check her emails. You see, you just have to analyze what you do and how you do it, so if something goes awry, you can detect the faulty part/behavior and fix it.

4) Once you have done 1), 2) and 3) then you can start to take the appropriate steps to prevent, or counter the attacks against you. How? Well, this chapter and the next are about that.

Let's recap according to Opsec, the process you just learned. The way of protecting yourself against attacks to your vulnerabilities begins with identifying what critical information you want to protect; secondly, by analyzing where the threats to that information you deem critical, may come from, like the environment or your devices. And ultimately, do something about it.

Ok, now on with our thing. I warned you that this was going to get geeky, so to make your reading and your life easier, I will only list for you now all the vulnerabilities, to let you go fetch a drink or some pizza before I go into the details of each vulnerability in the next chapters.

4.6
Vulnerabilities Outside of your electronic devices

The list:

1) Your passwords

2) Your messages (what you say, write or post with your electronic devices)

3) Your unattended electronic devices

Not many, but as you will read in the next chapter, they are enough to give you a headache.

4.7
Vulnerabilities Inside your electronic devices

The other list:

3) Your hard disk drive

4) Your browser

Not many either, but these are sufficient to leave you sleepless

Alright, let's do something about those external and internal vulnerabilities. But first, I promise you that I was going to give you some time to get a drink of water or to get a slice of pizza.

Well, what are you waiting for? Go get it. And then, turn to the next chapter.

Chapter 5:
Are you vulnerable from the outside to cyberparasite attacks?

As you read in Chapter 4, there are two main groups of vulnerabilities:

1) GROUP 1: **Outside** of your electronic devices

2) GROUP 2: **Inside** your electronic devices

Chapter 5 will be about the vulnerabilities coming from outside your electronic device, and how to counter them to prevent a hostile attack. Now we are going to business.

GROUP 1: Vulnerabilities outside your electronic device

I am going to do something for you. I am going to list again the most important of these vulnerabilities and then I will explain them to you in plain language, while providing you with tangible and doable solutions. There are many more vulnerabilities in this group, but I will address the most common and therefore, the most important ones.

1) Your passwords

2) Your messages (what you say, write or post with your electronic devices)

3) Your unattended electronic devices

5.1
Your passwords

Ok, you might say "I knew that. I saw it coming, it's all about my passwords". Then I ask you why you haven't done anything about it? Here is the thing. Whenever we register on-line for something like a service, a new web page, a club, a school, a bank, anything, we are usually asked to come up with an user-name and a password. And of course, since we are smart we come up with clever passwords, right? Well, let me tell you something.

It has been studied (so I read), that people tend to use easy-to-remember passwords (very clever, eh?), so next time they are at whichever site they enrolled or registered in, they can remember their password without pain (very clever too). For instance, some people, not you of course (wink, wink), use their names or their birth dates, or their pet's name, when prompted to come up with a password. And then those same individuals, not you of course (wink, wink, again), use the same password for everything in their virtual lives. They use it for their bank accounts, for their gym subscription, for their school transcripts, for their ATM transactions, you name it, they use that same password. Quite clever, ah? Not really, the passwords are the gateway to your critical information, the information you are trying to keep to yourself, away from the world.

A digital publication once listed the most common (and dumbest) passwords used, and they read something like this:

* 12345 or its counterpart, 54321

* password

* 11111 or 00000

* login

* yourname

* 5683 (for those curious, it spells L-O-V-E)

I know that you don't see yourself reflected in those common (but dumb) passwords. I know, you are smart. But sometimes smart people get tired too, and they begin to slack. So if your password(s) are not in the list above, great. But, one day you may feel tired and you may think that no one cares about your old self, much less your passwords, and you will start using, what I call other clever but "common" passwords.

There are many more than the list above, and yes, although we might think that they are clever, they are not really that clever:

* your spouse's name

* your child's name

* your pet's name

* the first digits of your identity card or your social security

* the last digits of your identity card or your social security

* the middle digits of your identity card or your social security

* your birthday

* your spouse's birthday
…

So, what is the solution to this nightmare of hard to remember passwords?
Well, check the next section.

5.2
Counter attacking lame passwords

Well, first you have to know two little secrets revealed by Edward Snowden.

But before I reveal Snowden's secrets, I have to tell you something.

Most cell phones today have a screen lock password. Also, most laptops, PCs, etc. have an initial password screen.
.
Let's talk about the cell phone screen lock. The password you are asked to provide is actually a clever pattern using your finger and the dots shown in your cell phone screen. The dots corresponds to the number 1 to 9 or 0 to 8. There you have three columns and three rows, or what the geeks call a
"3 x 3 matrix".

Usually the software manufacturer, in this example Android, asks you to draw a pattern with at least four points and using each point only once. Doing the math (which I didn't) that makes almost one million possible patterns to choose from. Don't choose the straight line pattern, or the typical "M" or "U". Be clever, and unleash your creativity, but be wise enough to have that pattern saved, just in case you forget.

You can bypass the pattern altogether, by choosing a PIN or a password that is more than eight digits or characters long.

Conclusion: use a strong and creative pattern to lock your screen, or even better, use a strong PIN or password of more than eight digits (at least 12-characters, you'll see why below).

Since we are at it, let me give you some tips for protecting that initial encounter with your cell phone, laptop, or electronic device:

a) when you start unlocking your device, try covering it as well as your gestures unlocking it, so no one, and I mean no one can see your unlocking pattern. It is very easy to observe your pattern from a distance without you knowing it.

b) if you feel unsafe using a finger pattern to unlock your screen, you may also change it for a password or a passcode.

c) in more modern devices you may substitute the lock screen pattern or the password option, by a different security feature, like fingerprint scanning or facial recognition.

My understanding, is that the lock screen patterns, fingerprint scanning and facial recognition are more prone to abuse from evil doers. I talked about the lock screen patterns already. If bad comes to worse, we have seen in movies that a fingerprint may be copied by various methods and then used to fool a scanner. Facial recognition, as of today, is a well developed feature, but prone to abuse like by using a photograph, or by a bad guy forcing the owner of the device to be recognized before taking control of the device.

My advise? I prefer passwords. However, you must know a thing or two about passwords, before you happily go around changing all your stuff.

5.3
Snowden's two little secrets

With that said, let me share with you a couple of secrets revealed by Edward Snowden. These secrets are not for the weak of heart.

Are you sitting down? If not, sit down, please.
est
Now that you are sitting down, I can reveal Snowden's first secret. Are you ready? Hold on to your chair, what you are about the read will literally blow your mind away. This is not about screen locks, it is about actual passwords, the same ones you use. You know, your clever passwords, the ones you use for your Facebook page, for your bank accounts, your cell phone unlocking (see above), etc., etc., etc.

According to RT.com and TheIntercept.com, Snowden explained that a computer can work out all the possibilities and crack your password in less that a second. Let me repeat that. In less than one second. Given that you use a common, eight-character password. You see, there are password dictionaries used by good and bad guys alike, which include permutations of common words (where the order of the letters is very important, for instance when you think that you can fool the computer by changing just one letter in your clever password, like "cleverly" using CaliforniO instead of California). Busted!

Conclusion: If allowed, always use passwords that are longer than eight characters. (Preferably 12 characters, you'll see why below)

Note to this conclusion: According to Snowden, a common eight character password can be cracked in less that a second. Now, hear this, according to Infosecurity-magazine.com, the Georgia Tech Research Institute found out that it would take more than 17,000 years to crack a 12-character password That is quite a long time. But not so fast. For the 12-character password to work properly, it has to come with a twist. That twist was revealed by Edward Snowden.

Are you ready for Snowden's second little secret? You think so? Ok.

So, this is the moment of truth, here is Snowden's second little secret: the twist to the 12-character password. In an interview conducted by John Oliver, and reproduced by RT.com, Snowden advised the general public to think differently with respect to passwords. He said that instead of thinking passWORDs we should think of passPHRASEs.

A **"passphrase"** is a sentence or a combination of words rather than a sequence of letters or a mere word, that substitutes a regular password. Since a passphrase is actually a sentence or a combination of words,and not just a word that might be found in password dictionaries, it increases the difficulty of cracking it down, while at the same time it makes it more convenient for you to memorize it. End result? More security for you.

Black hat hackers, the evil ones, are quite sophisticated, and they may use programs that try millions of tentative password combinations each second on the targeted system. That is what is called a **"brute force"** attack. So, by making the shift from 8-character or less passwords to 12-character passphrase ones, a "brute force" attack becomes much more difficult to run. Going from a less than a second crack down to a respectful 17,000 years chance of cracking your passphrase. Not bad.

But right now, even though it's for own security and privacy, I can hear you scream: "Twelve characters? That is crazy, how am I going to remember all that stuff, even if it's a sentence?"

Alright, alright I get you.

In your rescue, you may use one of the many methods available to create "passphrases". The trick consists that you should follow the accepted guidelines:

1) your passphrase should be long (12-characters or more) so it becomes difficult for anyone to crack

2) your passphrase should not come straight from a famous quotation, book, Bible, the movies, etc.

3) your passphrase should be unique for each device or situation that you encounter

4) your passphrase should not be intuitive, so not even your non-hacker Mom should be able to guess it

Lemme run by some examples, so you understand how to develop strong passphrases.

Example 1:
If you like Stars Wars, there is phrase used by Yoda:
"MayTheForceBeWithYou"
Now, can you tell me if this passphrase follows the guidelines listed above?
Let's see.
1) it is long alright, it has more than 12-characters, so this point is fulfilled.
2) this is a known phrase from a known movie, so this point is not fulfilled.
3) since it didn't cut the mustard in the point above, then this one is not fulfilled either.
4) if your best friend knows that your a Star Wars freak, he may be able to intuitively know that you are going to use that phrase. Busted!
Result: No, "MayTheForceBeWithYou" is not a strong, safe and reliable passphrase.

Example 2:
Another example. My12yoCatIsWhite.
Tell me if this passphrase follows the guidelines.
Let's check it:
1) it is long, it has more than 12-characters, check mark.
2) it is not a sentence coming from any known source, check mark.
3) if you are using it for just one of your devices, then it's fine, check mark.
4) it is intuitive only to you, who knows exactly that your cat is 12 years old, and it's black. Maybe, and maybe, your non-hacker Mom could sort of have guessed it. But I really doubt it.

<u>Result</u>: Yes, "My12yoCatIsWhite" is a strong, safe and reliable passphrase.

Well, we all have to develop a password management system.

<u>Example 3</u>:

Last example. And after this one, I think that you will get the hang of it, and become an expert "passphrase" maker.

Passphrase: Maym12yowcBeWithYou.

As you can see, this a combination of both passphrases above, making them work together, one weak and one strong, to provide an easy to remember but strong, safe and reliable passphrase.

Let's dissect it to understand it.

1) it is long. It has more than 12-characters. Pass.

2) although the Yoda phrase is very well known by Star Wars freaks and others, two words have been changed by the acronym of your pet's characteristics. So instead of "May The Force Be With You" you have cleverly changed it to "May My 12 Year Old White Cat Be With You". And to make it more complex you have only used the first letters of your pet's characteristics to make the passphrase stronger "May m 12 y o w c Be With You", which put all together reads "Maym12yowcBeWithYou". Pass.

3) if you are using it for just one of your devices, then it's fine. Pass.

4) although somewhat intuitive, only you hold the key to understand that "the force" is gone and that your "cat" has replaced it. Pass.

<u>Result</u>: Yes, it passed the test with flying colors. Congratulations.

So, there you have it. There are no more reasons to have lame passwords. Now you can have super strong passphrases. So, be a good sport and go find your own passphrases.

5.4
An alternate method to passphrases

Sometimes, you may want to use even more complicated passwords, without going the passphrase route. That is fine. You may want to invent whatever Martian looking password that does not mean anything, that you may wish.

You are just limited by your imagination, and by 90+ letters and symbols on your keyboard (26 of which are English alphabet letters). So, a password like &Ha"4/@M=#U\, may the thing for you. Like I said, that's fine. Just as long as you know what you are doing and can remember it too. Good for you.

We could say that this alternate method renders useless the common words and phrases dictionaries out there. Those weird looking characters make no sense to a computer dedicated to cracking passwords and passphrases, so a brute force attacks is out of the question.

Now, either you use passphrases, passwords or Martian looking passwords, you should have one for each case that you need one. One for your school, one for your bank, one for your gym (if you ever need one), one for your ATM card, one for your magazine subscription, one for everything that needs a password.

To create so many passwords, passphrases or Martian looking passwords you need to have a clever mind, ready to come up with one each time you are prompted to create one. And then, you have to use that same clever mind to remember each one and the place where you need each one.

Let me tell you, just creating so many complex passphrases, especially if you have just one 12 years old white cat, is a big mental enterprise. Let alone remember them for each case in particular. Just the thought of it, makes me dizzy.

Well, I have the solution for your nightmare: a Password management System.

Easy to say, buddy. But what is it?, you may say.

It's simple. Read the next section.

5.5
A Password Management System

A password management system is not your BF (best friend), whom you have entrusted with the amicable task of keeping track and recording all of your passwords, nicknames, user-names, and other sort of personal stuff. No, no. Don't mix friendship with passwords.

The "**password management system**" I am talking about is a service that allows you to generate random and complex passwords for you to use, and at the same time it allows you to store and retrieve those complicated randomly generated passwords at your own will.

In the previous section we concluded the following:

1) that an easy to remember password is not safe for your own security. Those passwords are too predictable and therefore easy to find.

2) that it is better to use more than eight-character passwords, preferably 12-characters.

3) that passphrases are better than passwords.

4) that randomly generated 12-character Martian passwords are very safe and reliable too

5) that you should have unique passphrases for each account that you have.

6) that you may go crazy trying to remember all of those passphrases

There are free and paid password management systems. Depending on the depth of your wallet you may go one route or the other. Some systems have password generators, so you have a 1-2 solution. The way they work is that the system manages your passwords in a secure way, meaning that you dump all your passwords and passphrases into one big vault, and you access them every time you need to use a password or passphrase. You lock and unlock your password vault with one master key.

If the systems has a password generator, then you can generate new passwords as you go along, storing them in you vault and then accessing them when you need them. Your information, or database, is usually encrypted, which is an additional plus for the system.

If you want to find the best or the top password management systems, even if you are loaded with cash, or you are penniless, run a Google search with these magical words "best **open source** password management systems" or "top **open source** password management systems". That simple. I mention the "**open source**" phrase instead of the word "free" because open source systems have accessible code that anyone can check and verify if they do what they claim to do. Free and paid password managers may be compromised by the same corporation offering the service. It is impossible to verify their real intentions.

Anyway, here is a list of password managers (note that some are open source, and some are not):
* Bitwarden: bitwarden.com (Open source)
* KeepassX: www.keepassx.org (Open source)
* TrueKey by Intel: www.truekey.com/ (NOT open source)

This chapter is getting too long, and we still have to cover some stuff that is very related to passwords.
So, let's have a break and we'll see each other in the next chapter.

Chapter 6:
More tools for you against lame passwords

Did you take a break? I did, so I'm ready.

Let's recap. Since last chapter we have been analyzing vulnerabilities from GROUP 1, i.e. those outside your electronic devices. We went over screen locks and passwords, and you also learned about passphrases and Martian passwords. I gave you a neat way to store and retrieve them too.

Now, we are going to get fancier (some would say geekier), and step this password privacy thing a notch.

You don't have to do this part, but I think that if you happen to be a politician, a head of state, a CEO, a famous star, someone who handles sensitive information, or if you happen to be just you, I would heartily encourage you to heed my advise here.

6.1
One more step

What you have learned so far is great stuff. In fact the majority of savvy electronic device users apply those good practices of 12-character passphrases, Martian passwords and the rest of the methods related to passwords, daily. Like drinking a glass of water. It's second nature.

But with all the news about snooping eyes, Internet fraud and digital crime, some very clever individuals came up another idea to protect us from criminals and snoopers. They devised an extra layer of security for you. The idea came about because technology has allowed the bad guys to become more sophisticated and break more easily into your usernames and passwords.

Let me clarify that this is not "just another" idea (like a gimmick), as I loosely mentioned in the paragraph above. It is a great idea.

Imagine that you have been asked to come to a party via a funny looking invitation that has an innocuous code printed on the back. Only those invited, like you, can go to the party. The day of the party, once you arrive to the venue, you are asked to provide your ID, to verify your age, and your name. The guard at the door, verifies in his list if your name is in it, and he visually checks you to see if you resemble the photo in your ID, and if your scanned fingerprint matches his records. After checking everything, he lets you in.

Now you are inside the place, but you don't see your buddies or a party environment. What you do see is a lot of people, so you check your funny looking invitation and it says that you have to go to the second floor and knock in the red door. So you go upstairs, and after your knocking someone show his face through a hole in the door, and asks you for your invitation. You give it to him, he verifies that the code printed on the invitation matches with the one he has in his list, he asks for your name to verify that it matches the code, he runs a biometric scan of your retina, and since all is Ok with you, then he opens the door.

You have finally made it to the party.

What I tried to explain you here is that although you may have access, via your ID and your name in a list, others may fake to be you and also enter your private party. But if the party is held upstairs, and the impostor does not have an invitation to know which door to knock, then he wont be able to enter the party impersonating you. And even if the bad guy tried knocking on all doors, he wouldn't be able to produce a funny looking invitation like yours, much less the unique code that is printed on it, or pass the retina scanning test. His evil behavior and intentions were avoided.

You avoided them by additional layers of security, in this case the funny looking invitation with its printed code, and the other biometric scans. So an impostor may enter, but not make it to the real party because he lacks the necessary tokens or proof to be allowed in.

Those additional layers of security are called Multi-factor authentication or MFA for short. In real computer life, you will not deal with humans, but rather machines, so no one, no human being will ask you through a hole in the door for anything. Instead, you will have an authentication system asking you to provide something that ONLY YOU know (that the party is upstairs), something that ONLY YOU have (the printed code on the funny looking invitation), something that shows that you are ONLY YOU (your ID and yourself), and a test to verify that you are actually ONLY YOU (the fingerprint and retina biometric scans).

The principle behind multi-factor authentication is based that someone other than you could not likely be able to produce all the stuff required by the system, and that ONLY YOU could do it.

For instance, if you had a double-factor authentication in place for your bank account or your Facebook page, then you would initially enter your account or page via your password or passphrase. At that moment the system would generate what is called a **"dynamic code"**, which is usually a one time-valid number sent to your cell phone or via email or by other electronic method, that you would have to enter when prompted. After doing so, then you would have access to your bank account or you Facebook page.

I think MFA is a good method to protect your privacy. It has some drawbacks, for instance the method implies that you have to have your cell phone with you at all times when you are accessing any place that requires it. For some that is not a drag, but you have to keep in mind that it also implies that you have to have a fully functional, charged cell phone, within the coverage area. That means that if your Dad is checking his bank account on his trip to the Sahara dessert where there may not be cell coverage, he will have difficulties retrieving his information. And if there was coverage or range maybe the extreme temperature would shut down his cell phone rendering it inactive for a while.

Some people don't like to use this extra layer of security claiming that SMS (or text messages) delivered to cell phones are slow by nature, that hackers may be able to intercept SMS messages. They also say that if your cell phone is lost or stolen then you don't have that extra protection. Hey, no one said it was perfect. But as of today, computer scientists are working to improve the two-factor authentication method to make it faster and more reliable.

There are other methods used for multi-factor authentication, in which you don't have to use SMS text messages. For instance, you can use Google Authenticator, or any open source Authenticator app. My point is that multi-factor authentication should be on your list of weapons against cyberparasites.

6.2
Your messages

If you recall, we are still in GROUP 1 of the vulnerabilities outside your electronic device.
We have already covered passwords, and I gave you Snowden's little secrets and the tips that you need to implement to have a strong and reliable password or passphrase.

The second most common vulnerability of this group is: your messages (what you say, write or post using your electronic devices).

I will repeat what I said in Chapter 4: "If you are one of the good guys, my advise to you is the following. If you don't want anyone to know that you are pondering into joining the bad guys, don't be one or don't do anything to become one. Just don't do it. So, that way you will not have anything to hide, and no one will find anything bad about you, because you actually never did it.

If you don't want anyone to know about it, don't do it.

Period".

That goes for your messages. If you are angry at someone and you send him a ranting message, that message will not go away. It will haunt you forever. If you think you are funny and you want to tell a joke deprecating certain group, same thing, if you send a message with it, that bad joke will haunt you forever.

Some times you may think that sending a picture is private or may be harmless. Well, let me tell you that if the picture gets into the wrong hands you are doomed, maybe for life.

You may think that by sending just once, your bank password to your friend, with a snapshot of your your monthly statement, nothing will happen, then you are in for a big surprise.

Nevertheless, you may have other information that you consider private and you don't want the world to make fun of you because of it (for instance that weird looking mustache your grandpa is using, or pictures of you when you were 13 years old, full of pimples, and with a finger up your nostril). It's understandable. But, what can you do?

The easiest initial step is to make all, and I mean ALL, your Internet profiles PRIVATE.
The next step require a little bit of help.
So, here comes Snowden to the rescue. Again.

In an interview with Micah Lee posted in theintercept.com in 2015, he said that phone calls and messages should be encrypted. And he even suggested a super easy to use app. I wont give you the name of it here, so you go and read Micah's excellent article in full, and if you really like it then subscribe. Go, Micah!

I know. I can read your mind. You are asking, what is encryption?

Well buddy, encryption is to information what a scrambled egg is to a regular egg. You have your information, messages, texts, etc. and you scramble them in such a way that no one, except you, the scrambler, can have access to it. In a few words, when you encrypt something, you are hiding it from others.

In computerese the scrambling process is called "**encoding**", the egg is called "**information or message**" or "**normalized data or plaintext**", and the one reading the message is called the "**authorized party**". With the process of encryption an otherwise intelligible message becomes pure gibberish, so everyone can hold it, read it, play with it, look at it, paint it, but no one can access the real meaning of the encrypted message, except the authorized parties.

The encryption process uses an series of instructions or an "**algorithm**" called "**cipher**" to scramble information into apparently random characters called "**ciphertext**". To decode the hidden message you need to use a special "**decryption key**", with which, as if it was magic, you can turn the random characters of ciphertext into nice looking plaintext.

There are many encryption methods, but the most widely used are:

1) Asymmetric or Public Key, and

2) Symmetric or Private Key

They are both based on the same principle explained above, but differ in their purpose or use.

Let's use an example. You and I want to communicate. How does it work with a Private and a Public Key?

In the Private Key encryption method, you and I have a decryption key to send encrypted messages. We both also use the same key to decrypt the message we send to each other. Very straight forward.

In the Public Key encryption method, let's say that you have a Public Key and that I have a Private Key. With your Public Key you can encrypt messages and send them to me. I can receive those messages and use my Private Key to decrypt and read them in plaintext.

However, with a Private Key I would not be able to encrypt a message and send it to you, nor would you with a Public Key be able to decrypt a message if I sent you one.

Summary:
1) Asymmetric or Public Key: Private reads (decrypts). Public sends (encrypts).
2) Symmetric or Private Key: Both, reads (decrypts)and sends (encrypts).

Pretty neat, eh?

The topic of encryption is very vast. In fact people could write stacks of books about encryption. But for this book I will just stop here.

Conclusion: read Micah Lee's article, and you should encrypt your messages. All of them.

6.3
Your unattended electronic devices

The last set of vulnerabilities in GROUP 1 is yours and yours alone. Your carelessness.

Let me explain.

You can physically leave your cell phone on top of your towel at the beach. And it can sit there and fry with the blazing sun, and maybe melt down. Or it can also be stolen. End of the story?

Not really. If you happen to be Kim you-know-who or Angeline-you-know-who, maybe the bad guy prefers not to steal your cell phone but rather install some sort of spy software, with the purpose of spying all your conversations, messages, photos, location, and so forth. And while you have all the paparazzi snapping pictures of you at the beach, a bad guy may be messing with your telephone without you noticing it.

My understanding is that if someone steals your cell phone, or installs in your cell phone some sort of spying mechanism, he is up to no good. It doesn't seem that he has good intentions. So the fact of leaving your device unattended is a major vulnerability.

Now, what if you attach your cell phone to your hand with duct tape, the silver one. And then, to make sure that no one steals it, you cover the duct tape and your hand with sticky super-glue or gooey crazy-glue. Now you're safe. Ha, they would have to chop your hand off if they wanted to steal your cell phone. End of the story?

Not really. Keep reading. Now you have absolute physical control of your cell phone. So you go around your school/office/movie-set proudly showing your ingenious idea of keeping your cell phone at a close distance to you. In fact VERY close distance. And then comes your BF. She tells you about a new app, a great one, so cool everyone is using it. It uses the latest technology to measure your body fat while matching it with your innate quantum healing power, to provide you with a number from 1 to 10 about your chances of winning the lottery every hour, allowing you to lose 1 pound after you have used it for a week. It even keeps a record and shows it to you in a graph! And the best of it: it's FREE.

Those words resonate in your brain,

B-O-D-Y F-A-T,
P-O-W-E-R,
W-I-N-N-I-N-G T-H-E L-O-T-T-E-R-Y,
L-O-S-I-N-G W-E-I-G-H-T,

but the one word that triggers your endorphins to the max, the word that resonates more in your brain is

F-R-E-E.

It means that if download this cool app, you won't have to run more errands at home to increase your allowance, or if you are an employee, you won't have to compromise your family's budget by spending on something unnecessary, but oh, so cool, or if you are movie or rock star, you won't have to spend a cent in an app that should be given to you for free anyway, hey you are the star.

So, like a mad man, you try download that app like there was no tomorrow. Your adrenaline is so pumped up that you don't have time to read the "**terms of service**" (those little, super little words that tell you what the app does, and some other legalese). You want it now. Bam! Done!. Now you have all that cool stuff. Just like the rest of the gang. So cooool! You feel sooo great.

And after a couple minutes you even forgot that you downloaded it.

You see, you do have absolute physical control over your cell phone, you even have it attached with duct tape (the silver one) and sticky glue to your own body. But you don't have complete control of your whims and likes. And what you just downloaded, albeit free, may have all the necessary code to easily spy on you. WITH YOUR OWN PERMISSION!

In my first app, PrivatBrowse, I set my terms of service clearly stating that no information about you or any user through my app was going to be collected. At least not by me. I gave it away for free, with no ifs, or catches or tricks. You should look for apps like that. And while you are at it, and you haven't downloaded it, do so. It will make your browsing faster than most other browsers and in complete privacy, like no other browser. If you have a grandma with an old cell phone, like I do, download it for her. She will have a blast and immediately notice the difference. Try it.

So, be aware. The word "free" is great, but it is also a great gimmick to lure you (unless it specifically tells you that there is no catch, like my app, PrivatBrowse). You may not pay a cent for something that is free, but you may pay for it in a different form unknown to you so far. You may be paying by giving up your personal information and data. And that personal data has a value in the market. Companies pay dearly for it because they can target advertising, offers, you name it, on you, and the rest whose data they bought. Creepy, isn't it?

There was a Canadian Broadcasting Corporation (CBC) program/documentary that I encourage you to watch, about how you can be spied on, without you realizing that you have approved all the spying.

Please don't get me wrong. I am NOT saying that this ordeal will happen to you. In fact, it may never happen to you.

My intention here is that you open your eyes, and be aware that technology has taken us places, but also it has created an extremely high dependence of us on such devices. And it is in your best interest to know the possibilities and also the limitations of technology.

So, if you think that your electronic device (cell phone, tablet, etc.) has been compromised, then it would be wise to do the following:

1) uninstall all applications that you don't recall downloading

2) sometimes spying apps are not simply observed. In this case, if after uninstalling suspicious apps you still fear that your device is compromised, then back up all of your information, and then reset your equipment to the initial factory settings. That way you wipe out all nefarious spying programs that you think you may have but that you can't see, and you can begin with a clean slate, as if nothing happened.

Conclusion: Use the best passphrases possible to prevent easy entry in your phone in case you lose it, or if your electronic device is stolen.

Try to keep your cell phone and other electronic devices close to you (don't need to use duct tape or super glue, though).
Verify what you download in app stores and on-line.
Do read the terms of service to see what you are getting into. Sometimes the word free doesn't mean free. You ultimately pay with either giving up your privacy or by paying with your personal data.
If you suspect you have been hacked, uninstall suspicious apps. If still feeling uneasy, back up your data and restore to factory settings.

Wao. We have finished the first part of the book. You now know about the possible vulnerabilities outside your cell phone or whatever device you're using, and how to defend yourself against cyberparasite attacks. I gave you the formulas to prevent those cyberparasite attacks from the outside to your stuff. In short, you have received the basic tools to safeguard your privacy. Heck, I have even given you some lingo to speak impressively at parties. Can't complain.

Next part is even cooler than the previous one. This next part separates the wanna-bes from the pros. The good thing is that it's easy to implement, you just follow the step-by-step guide in each of the coming chapter.

6.4
A word on Open Source

In Chapter 5 I introduced you to the term **"Open Source"**. But, what is Open Source?

Well, it is usually referred to software whose original source code is free, and that it can be distributed or modified for free. Sometimes you can see the term FOSS, which is short for Free Open Source Software. Same thing.

The term free here refers to the license to the software. That is like saying that the person or group of persons that spent resources, time and manpower to develop a great software, and have the legal rights to it, some day decide that for the good of mankind, they want to release their software for everybody for free, and that anyone can change or distribute it like they please. So they surrender their rights and give license to the world to use their great software.

Open Source is mistaken by free software. Open Source really means that the source code is available to the general public with no restrictions in the use and modification of the original code.

To make an analogy, an Open Source pizza is one which you know where it came from, you know exactly its original components and ingredients, and one that you can freely mix it yourself and freely distribute it to others, or that you can freely add more flavors to it or freely take away some, as you please. All in the open, no hidden nothing. The users are consider co-developers of the pizza and therefore they have access to the source ingredients or components of the pizza. And it's free.

A free pizza, is one which you may not know where it came from, of which you don't know exactly its original components, one that you cannot mix or distribute or modify as you please. One pizza in which you are only considered as a user, a mere pizza aficionado, so no ingredients are revealed to you. But it's free. Sometimes that free pizza comes after you have given some information about yourself or after you have watched something the pizza provider wants you to watch.

See the difference?

Some fantastic Open Source Softwares that I personally use are Linux, Firefox, VLC media player.

Maybe after reading this, you may contemplate start migrating from your current paid programs to some Open Source Software. It's a thought. Just think about it, they may enhance your privacy (wink, wink).

Chapter 7:
Vulnerabilities Inside your electronic devices

Although the list is short, and seemingly harmless, once you uncover the details of it, you will see the world in a different way.

The most common vulnerabilities inside your electronic devices are:

1) Your hard disk drive

2) Your browser

7.1
Your hard disk drive

I realize that the words "hard disk drive" have become so common use in our language that they are almost the computer equivalent of "peanut butter and jelly".

However, I also realize that for someone foreign to computerese, the words, although heard and maybe even used commonly, they may still be generate some sort of allergy to hear. Like the people who have allergy to peanuts. If that is you, don't feel bad, I understand you.

Let's start from the beginning. The **"computer"** is a fine piece of equipment which, once instructed via **"programs"**, allow us, humans, to perform **"logical tasks"** at lightning speed. The programs are a set of commands that the computer follows to perform certain operations. The logical tasks are mathematical in nature and they may be as simple as adding 2 + 2, and as complex as determining the probable path that hurricanes take in their way by the Caribbean Sea.

Are you still with me? OK.

Some examples of computers? Well the ubiquitous PC, your friend the smart-phone, your laptop, your tablet, your graphing calculator, and today, we could say that even washing machines and most electronic devices have some sort of computer inside. Yep.

The computers have guts inside them, just like us. Remember my early experience with one of them in Chapter 1? They also have other devices around them, like mouses, printers, etc., but we are not interested in them right now. We are going to focus in the guts and the programs that run those guts.

What are the internal organs of a computer that are of interest to us? Its brain and the memory. The rest can wait for someone else's book.

The brain is commonly known as the **"CPU"** (short for Central Processing Unit) and it manages the rest of the computer components. The CPU is contained in a spider like computer chip called the **"microprocessor"**. By feeding the computer brain with instructions, it can work by reading them and doing what it is told, like to type a letter that you write, to perform the calculations for your physics lab, to view the pictures from last weekend's party, to read emails, to download documents, etc.

Geeks in parties brag about their CPUs by comparing their speeds, which is the number of calculations their CPU can make in a second, normally counted in billions. The faster the speed of the processor the more calculations that can be executed. Hence the bragging rights.

Now, to function properly and mimic us, the brain has to have a memory. And like us, the computer brain has a long term and a short term memory. The long term memory is embedded into each computer and it's called "**ROM**" or read-only memory. Short term memory is called "**RAM**" or random-access memory, and it helps the brain to wok seamlessly doing calculations, crunching numbers and performing logical tasks, as if there was no tomorrow. But all used data is completely forgotten from the RAM part of your computer brain when you turn it off.

Even though I compared both memories, human and computer, as very similar organs, they differ in something very important. Human memory is good at forgetting, but computer memories don't forget.

And to make that difference even greater, computer memory is aided and abetted by its accomplice, the "**hard disk drive**", which is an auxiliary memory that keeps all information and data safely stored, ready to be retrieved, and it does not disappear like the RAM memory even if the computer is turned off.

To recap, you can say that the CPU does all the thinking, processing, and calculating, and you can also say that the hard disk drive gives the computer its power to remember whatever you feed to it.

Hugo Alejandro Cuenca

So, where are you party photos? In the hard disk drive. Where is the data from that report you turned in last week? In the hard disk drive. Where is your Word Processing software? In the hard disk drive. Where is your browser, the one you use to surf the Internet? In the hard disk drive. Where are all your documents from school or work? You said it, in your hard disk drive.

Therefore, in view of the preceding, it is is obvious that your hard disk drive is one of the vulnerabilities of your electronic devices. It is so important that it has become the target of attacks.

You see, there are black hat hackers working on their own or for some government or corporation , developing pieces of code to maliciously infiltrate into your devices. Their purpose could be:

1) to damage your computer (or computers in general of all of us)

2) to snoop and spy on you

3) to do evil things against you

4) all of the above

And most of the time they do it by penetrating your hard disk drive.

But, how do hackers do it? Let's go to the next section.

7.2
Why is your hard disk drive vulnerable to cyberparasite attacks?

Because it can be easily infected. When you install the wrong program, or when you download a file without knowing that it is malicious, or if you inadvertently download an infected document or even a picture that has a malicious code, you are allowing others to have a front seat with a panoramic view of what you do, where you bank, what messages you send or receive.

You get the point?

OK, now let's move to the practical part. How to protect yourself, and guts inside your laptop.

7.3
How to protect your hard disk drive

If you know that you are prone to leaving unattended computers, cell phones and other electronic devices out in the open, then YOU KNOW, that one day someone will steal your device. That is a fact of life.

But if you don't know that someone may break into your home/room/dorm/office, then you may be for a surprise when you find that your always well protected device was stolen.

And since your hard disk drive is intrinsically attached to your device, you will lose that too.

So, bye, bye photographs, and all those pictures of you in your Sponge-Bob-Square-Pants underwear, or the love letter you meant to send to your would-be girlfriend, or the funny pictures of your teacher surrounded by mean looking students when he fell asleep in the bus when going to the museum.

Bye, bye your privacy.

OK, since you were honest enough to admit that your are sometimes careless (and I know we all are) with your devices, I will give you a solution.

But first, let's read another case.

You can be the President of the greatest superpower on earth, or the humblest of all human beings, but one day you will see yourself in the position that you have just received an email or you have just visited a web site that everyone's talking about, and you have to open the message or download a file that explains a secret that you didn't know. Or you plug to your device your BF's flash drive so you can see the fantastic photos he shot last weekend at the pool party.

And, wham! You just have opened the doors of your computer to criminals, or to fastidious marketing corporations that follow each of your steps and that sell your data, or you just have fallen into the trap of massive government surveillance programs. Whichever is your case, Mr President of the Greatest Superpower on Earth or Mr. humblest of all men, you're doomed. As well as those around you with whom you share the great message you received, or with whom you share that fantastic downloaded document that explains the secret you didn't know. Or those to whom you send those wild pool party pictures.

You now have someone following your footsteps through your own GPS, or reading your email or text messages, or snooping on your documents, files, letters, and photographs, or following you in the Internet, or embezzling you out of your hard earned allowance cash without you even thinking that someone is doing it.

Well, all of those are cases of extreme intrusion in your privacy.

My solution to avoid the consequences of you (us) being careless, is to encrypt your (our) information that is stored in your (our) devices.

Mind you, there are things that encryption protects and things that it doesn't.

7.4
How to encrypt your hard disk

I live in a country where there are robberies, and houses and apartment are broken into. So, placing fences around the perimeter of a house is seen as normal, as well as placing bars in all windows. The purpose is the protection of the people and things that may be inside. Ugly but pretty nifty.

Your hard disk drive is like one of those Venezuelan houses that may broken into, but if you have your fence in place and the window bars, you and your property will be better protected. If you use encryption in your hard disk drive, you will breathe more peacefully.

One thing, though. Fences and bars protect Venezuelan homes to a certain extent. But, if the thieve trying to break in is a real pro, well, maybe the homeowners will have an issue, fences or not.

With your hard disk drive happens the same thing. There are certain things that you will protect, but there are others that you wont.

I spoke earlier about your leaving your laptop at a desk or an airport and having it stolen due to carelessness or because someone snatched it from you. Well, if that happens to you, you lost your entire computer, hard disk drive included. However, if you encrypted your disk, then your files (documents, photos, songs, videos, etc.) wont go to the evil guy.

As you see, I'm talking about the physical device, but not yet when you send text messages, surf the Internet or use your cell phone. That is game for another section here.

In order to encrypt your hard disk drive, you have to know what operating system your computer runs. There are mainly three, and I'm sure that you fall into one of those categories.

Your operating systems may be:

1) Linux based

2) Windows based or

3) Mac based

So, go and find it, and then come back. No, just kidding. I'm positive that by now just by looking at the back of your PC or

Laptop you now see that it has a half bitten apple, or in the front it has a colored window as if moving. Apple the first, Windows based the second, get it? Ok.

For Linux, which is one of my favorites, you either installed it yourself, so you already know your operating system, or another 16 year-old kid just like me installed yours. You may call him up, ask him.

7.5
Linux encryption
(for those using Linux as their operating system)

If you or that 16 year-old kid installed a Linux based operating system in your PC, you will have to either re-install it yourself, or call the little geek to re-install your OS ("operating system") again. Linux only lets you do it at the onset but not later. The standard Linux disk encryption is called LUKS.

So call the computer whiz and tell him these very same words:

"Hi (his name here), I am calling you because I wanted to do a back up of all my data, and I want to use the same Linux based OS you installed for me before. Can you drop by later today, please?" (always say please, regardless of the age).

This way your geek friend will show up with all the tools to do a back up, which is what you need to do to reinstall Linux. Now explain him that you read in a book from a famous computer expert and author (my name here) that what you want to do is to encrypt your disk. And that can only be done by first backing up all your data, and that you want to be present when he is doing the re-installation, because one of the first installation screens asks for a security key, and you want to be the one inputing such key.

The kid will be amazed at your newly acquired knowledge, so he'll gladly show you the screen with the Linux prompt "Choose your security key".

At this point you have to bear in mind two things:

1) You HAVE TO use a passphrase rather than a password, just like I taught you in the chapter 5, section 5.3, about passwords and passphrases. Go check it now. You will use this passphrase every time you turn on your computer, if you don't input it when prompted, your computer wont let you in.

2) If you lose your security key or passphrase you will also lose your data forever. Why? Because you have just encrypted it, and if you forget the passphrase, no one, and I mean NO ONE will be able to decrypt it, but you. Understood?

I have read that some really privacy-oriented people commit to memory their passphrases. If that is you, fine. I have also read about people writing down their passphrases and then securing the paper or notebook where they write all their stuff. If that is you, that's fine too.

Just keep in mind that if you belong to the first type of people but you tend to forget where you placed your keys, then it would be unwise to trust just your memory capacity. In the other hand, if you belong to the second group of people, and you tend to leave your paperwork all over, and you don't keep it to yourself, then you may have to re-think the way your maintain your privacy. I am not pointing fingers, I am just saying!

After you finished with the security key, then move on, with the kid reinstalling your Linux, to another screen that asks for your name, user name and a password to log in (I think I don't have to go over passphrases again, right?). The point here is to have you type a password/passphrase every time you start the computer (different from the security key). Please DON'T choose the option "Log in automatically" or you will defeat all the security measures your doing.

7.6
Windows encryption
(for those using Windows as their operating system)

If you have the cheap-o bare-bones Windows version you don't get BitLocker, which is a special Windows designed encryption system to protect your data. If you have the premium pay-through-you-nose version of Window, you do.

If you don't have BitLocker in your Windows system, don't cry. Just pay for an upgraded version so you can feel safer. And stop crying.

If you upgraded your Windows version, after the crying, or if you already have BitLocker, then go to your hard disk drive(the one marked as" C") and turn BitLocker on. This is done by right clicking "C" and then selecting the corresponding option.

There is a prompt that lets you have access to your disk, if you happen to be kicked out of your own system, God forbid. This "recovery key" as they call it, may help you in case of panic. At the end, you will be asked to restart, and when it does, the hard disk drive encryption process will begin. When finished, you may include an additional authentication step at startup. But this part is better done by your new friend, the 16year-old geek. After some time he will ask you if your prefer to use a USB drive or a Pin number to unlock your hard disk drive when turning it on. It's up to you to select either option. Ask your geek buddy what he thinks is better. If I were you, I would choose a Pin number instead of a USB drive. That way you exercise your memory or write another line in your notebook of passwords.

7.7
Mac encryption
(for those using Mac as their operating system)

Just like Windows, Mac has it own disk encryption system. It's called FileVault, and it is located in the Security and Privacy part of your system preferences. Just turn the option on, and presto, you're ready to go.

As before, you will be asked to create a recovery key in case you have amnesia and you locked yourself out of your computer. You should commit that number to memory or write it in you special password/passphrases notebook. Remember, this recovery key will allow you to unlock your hard disk drive.

At the end, and like Windows, you will be asked to restart your computer so the encryption process may begin.

Done. Pretty easy, ah?

7.8
How to encrypt your messages
(for those sending and receiving messages via cell phone)

We live in a society that is interconnected to such an extent, that I think Descartes famous "Cogito ergo sum" (I think, therefore I am) proposition, is quietly moving to "Tweet ergo sum" (I tweet, therefore I am), understanding the tweeting as an expression of our extensive involvement in social networks.

So, talking about cell phone calls and text messages, you should IMMEDIATELY use an alternate method to have them also encrypted.

What do experts recommend? Signal. It's a free App that you can download right now. Have everyone, and the dog download it. NOW. If you do, and then follow a simple step of initially authenticating both ends of the communication (you and your friends) you can rest assured that your messages will be encrypted and therefore unreadable by the evil guys.

If you're familiar with texting and messaging using apps like WhatsApp, then it would be easier for you to use Signal, because it's almost the same. But encrypted. And they don't collect your data.

To recap, heed the experts' advise: use Signal

7.9
Now that you have encrypted your hard disk drive, what happens with your Internet surfing?

As I have been telling you since page one, if you apply all the security and privacy protection measures that I have here explained to you, you will have done nothing if you are careless about what you do on the Internet, including sending and receiving emails.

Why? Because the Internet works like a Trojan horse, in all the sense of the word, to sneak into your "secured" system. And once a virus, a piece of code, or something malicious has entered your electronic device, you are DOOMED. All the time spent on encryption, learning about passphrases and the rest of the stuff, has been lost.

So, extra measures have to be taken in this case of Internet surfing.

Let's analyze together the most common cases. Of course, there are many more, but I think these are the usual ones that show up more frequently when you're surfing the Net.

1) Ads

2) emails

3) http

4) the net itself

Since these topics require considerable thought, I will explain each one in detail in the next chapter.

I have to warn you that if you thought the last couple of chapters were geeky, the next one will be a little more. However, you HAVE TO at least skim through it, so you are in better position to tackle your concerns about privacy.

My word of advise is this: If you have come all this far, and you have already visited the places I gave you and fetched all the tools that I have indicated, then you now have an arsenal of weapons ready to be used. But they are useless without ammo.

Next chapter will give your the ammunition to load those electronic slings shots, and virtual bazookas, so you become ready to fight the battle to earn back your privacy.

Let's go, amigo!

Chapter 8:
Vulnerabilities while surfing the Internet

I will never tire to repeat "It's a jungle out there", when talking about the Internet. The pray? You and I, and the rest of unsuspecting people using it.

There are various forms of being attacked by cyberparasites while on the Net:

1) Ads

2) emails

3) http

4) the net itself

8.1
Attacks coming from Advertisers

You see, you and I are potential customers, potential spenders, potential buyers, potential compulsive buyers, and the companies and the marketers are eager to push their products on us. But to do so they have to know us better. They have to know where we go, were our parents shop, where we shop, what type of places we go, what kind of people we associate with, what kind of words we use in our messages, etc.

So, when you are aimlessly surfing the Net and land in a place, your computer is forced -fed with a cookie. That innocent looking cookie is just a code or a file sent from that website where you landed that gets stored in your "browser". "**Browser**" is the program that allows you to surf the Web.

Once in your browser, the cookie starts gathering information about you. What was your activity in the page, what did you download, what did you click, and also it records what places have you visited before.

Cookies are also used, by legitimate enterprises, to register information that is only yours, and that you willingly provided, such as your name, your password to the site, your banking information if you purchased something. The security of these cookies depend on the site that issued them and forced-fed your computer with it, and of your browser.

There are tracking cookies too, which record your private browsing history, without you even knowing it.

Advertisers use what is called third-party cookies, which are hidden in websites in the form of banners or external websites. When you innocently click on them, or just by the ads being there, you open your browser's history to advertisers, so they can cater the products that are more relevant to the type of surfing you are doing.

However, I have a good word about advertisers: most of them are good people trying to make a living. They use the latest technology to make a nicer, luxurious living squeezing the last dollar from your and my data. Without advertisers some news companies, some sites would not exist. Youtubers would be marauding the streets, doing all sort of odd jobs, trying to maintain an expensive video hobby.

But advertisers come to the rescue and news companies, some sites and Youtubers begin to make money and become millionaires in their own right.

The problem is when they or the marketing companies they hire overextend themselves and start to gather more information from you than it's necessary.

How do you stop cookies from snooping on you? Well, this is a tough one. You have the option of opting out altogether. But disabling the good cookies causes login pages not to work. But if you insists, here is how to obliterate all the cookies (good and bad): In your browser, go to the Privacy and Security tab, which is usually in Internet options or preferences, then select Advanced Settings, depending on your browser, and immediately block whatever is related to cookies, first-party, third-party, or others. You may have to un-check the mark that says Accept cookies by default. Some browser say something like "Override automatic cookie handling".

You have another option, and that is to download "Privacy Badger" from the good guys at EFF. Their ad blocker doesn't just block any old add, it detects cookies with what they call "objectionable behavior" and if the cookie you have been sent from a domain continues to collect unique identifiers from you after the good guys have told them not to, then this sophisticated browser add-on stops advertisers from sneaking on you.

If you think you have cookies in your browser, and I'm sure you do have a bunch of them, go again to the History tab of your browser, and click "Clear recent history", then select the dates from which you want to delete cookies, and click "Clear everything". Before you clear other data, expand the history items to verify that you are not clearing other more important data.

Done.

If you want to go a step further and you happen to have Google Chrome or Firefox, you can also take advantage of a FREE add-on called AdBlock. First you go to the Chrome web store, then you look for AdBlock Plus, and down load it. Don't be fooled by other apps trying to use a similar name like AdBlock 2017 or AdBlock2018, they are copycats. Once you have downloaded it, you're ready.

In theory, although safe, Google Chrome has the know-how to grab your data and run. At the end of the day, Chrome is not Open Source and it's owned by Google, which lives and feeds itself from data.

If you wish, you may switch to Firefox, also free but Open Source, so there are no hidden codes secretly snatching your data. Download the same extension, similar to AdBlock and you are good to go. Atta-boy!

8.2
Attacks coming to your cell phone

If you have an old cell phone like my Grandma, or if you have a super-intelligent device, you know that you can also surf the web from the comfort of your own cell phone.

Want to have privacy? I heartily encourage you to use the best, ahem, browser in the world. Autographs at the end, please. Modesty aside, I designed, developed and published FREE, just for you buddy, a super fast browser, that has an extraordinary feature no other has. It does not store anything in memory (NO local cache from data or history ever saved). After you're done browsing, it cleans itself and erases all traces of your whereabouts.

Here are some of the comments you may read in the Google Store:
"Flat out fast and private..."

"FANTASTIC, very useful app for all"

NICE... better than other browser"

"Best application on android platform"

To be honest about how I came up with PrivatBrowse (that's the name of the browser, which you can download for free in the Google Store), I have to tell you a story.

Grandma was having issues with her oldie cell phone while surfing the Net. Since she is usually short on cash, she didn't have the means to buy a new phone. So I had an idea of creating a program, so light, that it could help her browse the Internet without having her cell phone crash every second.

The by-product of PrivatBrowse, is the privacy it gives to the users. You can use it in old phone technologies because the browser is extremely light, parallel to none in the market today. It is super-fast, and in comparison speed tests with renowned browser, it came ahead of the crowd by an ample margin.

To enhance the privacy part, I recommend that you use it along with privacy-friendly search engines such as Duck-duck-go. They don't store your date either.

Here is the place where you can download PrivatBrowse for FREE:

* jonathan-apps.com

* play.google.com (Search for it under: PrivatBrowse)

Well? What are you waiting for? Go get it!

8.3
Differences between Chrome Incognito and PrivatBrowse (my App)

Some people have asked me, why should they download my App when they have Incognito Browsing in Google Chrome.

The answer is multi-faceted (that word is for my English Lit teacher):

Google is a great company. I love Google, but it has an enormous appetite for data. If you let it run free it may even get know your potty times.

PrivatBrowse is not owned by a huge corporation such as Google, it's owned by me. Yes, humble me. And I can assure you, with a hand in my heart, that I don't have the least interest to collect any data from you or anybody. Much less potty times.

PrivatBrowse has a unique feature. It never gives any site permission to the use of your cell's camera, your microphone, your files, your location, etc. Those are your and your to use.

PrivatBrowse allows login information to be saved, even when you close your tabs, while still clearing cache and cookies. You may conveniently clear logins directly from the menu.

PrivatBrowse is faster. One journalist asked me at a Radio Station, how could I describe being faster with PrivatBrowse. Here I share with you what I told him on the air: "Have you ever been in a sail boat? Have you ever felt the salty air hitting your face while you catch the wind with your spinnaker? That is ultimate freedom, that is what it feels to surf the Internet with PrivatBrowse".

PrivatBrowse is also lighter. It is about 10MB, which is much, much less than regular browser.

Convinced now? Well? What are you waiting for? Go get PrivatBrowse!

You can download PrivatBrowse at: jonathan-apps.com
and at: play.google.com/store and look for PrivatBrowse

8.4
Attacks coming from innocent looking emails

Let's say you are an adult and it is one of those days, when you are paying the bills to pay, running errand, and your 16 year-old kid is pestering you about some computer thing. And then you get that email from you bank, saying that due to security reasons you have to verify your account, or that security has been breached and that your account is compromised.

So, you stop paying the bills, you re-schedule your errands, and you tell your son to wait, while you click that link in the email, to save the last few bucks you have in your account. Well, you have just been another victim of a phishing attack. Someone, somewhere, is getting access to your bank account, or just introduced a malware or virus into your computer.

What do you do to prevent these type of attacks? Here are a few tips:

1) verify who is sending you the email. If you see "Banc" instead of Bank, or "Finnancial" instead of Financial, or any other typo of typos or grammatical errors, be cautious. You may be in the verge of being phished.

2) in the same verification, if you receive and email such as "alertfromStateBank@gmail.com" or yourfinancialadvuisorBankUS@mail.suspicious-

site.etracker.com", be cautious too. Not because of the phony bank name I used as an example, but because if they were real banks the would not send emails from Yahoo, Gmail or any other service like those. It would have to come from the same bank.

3) when you receive a suspicious link in a email, DON'T CLICK IT right away, sometimes just hovering over it can show that what was written as an innocent looking link like www.TheBestBankintheWorld.com is nothing but a predator trap waiting for you in www.IwanttoStealyouDoughNOW.trackomatic.com. Needless to say, don't click it.

Another form of infesting your PC is through attachments that may carry viruses or malwares. Sometimes those viruses come in the same suspicious emails, some other times they may come from known sources that don't really know that they are spreading a malware.

4) another trick up your computer sleeve is through a little secret, that I'm gonna let you in

8.5
Ready to play like a kid?

When I was a kid, I mean a real kid, the kind who goes to the kiddy rides and barfs profusely after swinging like a maniac in the park, I used to play in a place full of sand, correctly named the sandbox.

Sandboxes were designed in a rectangular or square shape, surrounded by timber logs, that prevented the sand from moving anywhere. You could bring your toys in, but it was not fun to take any sand out.

The purpose of the sandbox was to isolate the kids inside, from the rest of the park, avoiding their use of the swings, the titter-totters, and other fun paraphernalia that the park had to offer. It could mean, implicitly, that if you were inside the sandbox you were a little kid.

You can apply the same principle in your computer through a virtual sandbox. A sandbox environment is a program that separates your confidential documents, files, etc. from the documents, files, etc. that you want to download but that you are not that sure about the source. What a sandbox environment does is to force a wall, like the timber logs in the kid's sandbox, between the document you want to open from unverified sources, and your computer. This way you risk nothing from the data, programs, files that you currently have and use in your PC.

Sandboxes can come in two forms:

1) Computer sandbox and

2) Cloud sandbox

The first one refers to the program that you download in your computer. The second makes use of the isolated environment provided by the cloud, like Google Drive.

Cloud is NOT as secure as a Sandbox.

Pretty good, ah? There are some free sandbox services out there, and here is a list:

a) Qubes: www.qubes-os.org (Open source)

b) Sandboxie: www.sandboxie.com (NOT open source, for Windows)

c) Shade: www.shadesandbox.com (NOT open source, for Windows)

My favorite? Qubes, because it's open source, and it's recommended by Snowden.

8.6
What is https?

When you open a search engine, like Google, or my favorite Duck-duck-go, there is a little rectangular window at the top, where you enter the site that you are planning on visiting.

If you look closely, it has some letters like so: http or https. Some have the word "Secure" and a locked padlock, or "Not secure" and an open padlock.

Well, "http" is a protocol for transmitting data over the web. When you surf the web, you may use http while visiting some web pages.

However http is insecure and the communication between you and the web page can be intercepted. That is, it has no encryption.

On the other hand, "https" (look at the little "s" at the end) is a protocol that is encrypted. Most websites now use https, or at least they should.

Good https is secure. It means that anything that you send to or receive from a web page will not be seen or spied by anyone else, except you and the site itself, but it cannot be interfered with.

https is not magic by itself, the site you are visiting and exchanging information with, may be sharing that same information you gave them, with somebody else. Therefore, a rule of thumb is always to make sure that you actually trust the site to begin with.

The question is: How do you make your browser automatically connect to a https connection when the site offers it? And the answer is: Download the add-on HTTPS Everywhere for Firefox. Presto.

8.7
The Internet and VPNs

This is a broad field. I already explained to you the cookie experience. So, I'll concentrate more on how to prevent being watched all the time, specially if you live in a country under totalitarian regimes.

Here the answer is to use something called a VPN, short for Virtual Private Network. VPN is a service that lets you connect to the Internet via a secure VPN server. .

But let's not get ahead of ourselves. When you are at home or you are in your office, if you want to connect to the Internet, you first do it through your ISP or Internet Service Provider. They let you visit the website you are interested. So, whatever you do, and visit goes first through your ISP, and they can spy on what you do and where you go.

The benefits of surfing using a VPN are twofold:

A. Benefits with respect to the prying eyes of your country's totalitarian regime
If your ISP happens to be a government run service, then all your searches about freedom, freedom of speech, and similar topics can lead you to receive a knock in your door coming from a bunch of guys with machetes and hand guns ready to beat you up.

However if you use a VPN service, your initial connection is with your VPN provider and it is encrypted. What that means is that your data moving between your computer and the VPN server can only be seen by your VPN server, and not the prying eyes of your totalitarian regime.

The result of all this is that your totalitarian ISP will not be able to see your encrypted data, therefore it couldn't really know what is your Internet activity. The only thing that it knows is that you are connected to a VPN server.

B. Benefits with respect to your privacy once on the Internet
Once you're surfing via a VPN server, the Internet thinks that you're located in the country where the VPN server is located. Most VPNs have multiple locations to choose from, so you can decide to be in a different city or a different country every day of the week, or how your mood decides.

If your totalitarian government wants to spy on you, they will only be capable of tracking you back to the VPN server. So, you real IP address remain hidden to all, except the VPN service provider. Also, if you land on a page that wants to track you down, it will only not be able to see your true IP address but the one from your VPN.

A small warning. When you use your VPN you will immediately notice that your connection will slow down. That happens because of all the encrypting taking place and the longer route taken now by your data when passing through the VPN servers.

But it is a small price compared to the privacy benefits you get.

Here is a list of VPNs for your consideration. Please verify their cost, speed, the location of their servers, the number of devices you can connect simultaneously, and other factors.

According to PC Magazine, an article by Max Eddy, rated these as their top best paid VPN performers:

a) NordVPN: www.nordvpn.com

b)KeepSolid VPN Unlimited: www.keepsolid.com

c) TunnelBear VPN: www.tunnelbear.com

d) TorGuard VPN: www.torguard.net

e) Golden Frog VyprVPN: www.goldenfrog.com

8.8
What is difference between a VPN and a proxy?

The main difference is that your VPN encrypts all you do, and it replaces your ISP by their VPN server. A proxy server is just a dedicated computer that acts as a mid-point between you and the place you're visiting. No encryption included.

The similarity between a VPN and a proxy is that both let you transmit the idea that you are connecting to the Internet from a different location (IP swap).

If you are just doing menial things you are Ok with a proxy. But if you deal with very sensitive information, you better go for a VPN.

If you happen to be in a cyber-cafe, the airport or other similar place that offers WiFi, your best bet is to go with a VPN to prevent the evil guys from stealing your data.

8.9
A word of two about TAILS and TOR

At he end of this chapter I wanted to include two additional powerful tools for your arsenal of weapons to protect your privacy.

If you feel that you've had enough, cool, you may end your reading now. You got yourself an A+.

However, if you are a geek at heart, this last part may bring some more knowledge in your quest for privacy, and it may open your mind to more possibilities in the world of cybersecurity.

Let's handle each powerful tool in its own section.

8.10
The secret about TAILS

You may have Windows or Mac or Linux as your operating systems. Well, TAILS is also a fully functional operating system. But its advantage over the others is that TAILS is designed to be used from a USB flash drive or a DVD, with total independence from your computer's original operating system.

Let's imagine you are a journalist in a conflict area or, a journalists trying to report from within a totalitarian state that chops the heads off of those against it. How do you send your information without losing your head, literally?

Here comes TAILS. You start a computer, any computer, the one at the hotel you're staying, insert your USB flash drive or DVD, and off you go to do your reporting. When you finish and you close TAILS, there is no trace of you doing anything in that computer.

How does it do it? Well, TAILS was designed to not use the host's computer hard disk drive, and you already know all the issues with hard disk drives that we went over in the preceding chapter. The beauty of TAILS is that it uses only the computer's RAM, which is erased immediately when you shut down the computer.

Now, if you use TAILS to work documents and send/receive emails, then it is wise also to encrypt them using the open source encryption programs available that I mentioned in other chapters.

If you're messaging then use Signal or other encrypted form of communication.

If you feel safe where you are, you may save your documents, files, photographs, etc. to a different USB flash drive, or even an external hard disk drive, that you have previously encrypted. Since TAILS is Linux based, it is wise to use LUKS, the same you used for your computer's hard disk drive.

TAILS is free, so you can download it at their site, and follow their instructions to install it.

One thing, TAILS relies on Tor to protect your privacy. So it would be good to use Tor as your browser if you are using TAILS.

You can get TAILS at: tails.boum.org

8.11
The secret about Tor

Tor is a free software that splits up your traffic or visit over several places on the Internet. By working this way, Tor distributes your data packets among several servers, and not one single link can be attributed to your destination. If someone or a company could see one of those points, they wouldn't be able to track down the source or the destination of your footprints. In addition to it, Tor changes the circuit connections every ten minutes or so, making it even harder to link your earlier data packet with the new one.

Tor actually is dedicated to protecting the transit of your data, but it doesn't make you invisible. For that, you have to implement additional measures.

Since Tor has been in the limelight due to some high profile cases, I think it's important to explain who uses Tor:

1) the bad guys. It ain't nothing you can do about it, there are always rotten apples.

2) the good guys also use Tor. Like human rights activists, people under an oppressive regime that bans the use of certain websites, freedom seekers, Journalists, whistle-blowers from government or corporations, those trying to protect themselves from ISPs that sell their data to marketers. And many more.

However, as any other toll, if you engage in the use of Tor, you have to do it responsibly, and with a kosher objective in mind. If you don't, then belong to the first group, the bad guys, and you should quit reading this now, and turn yourself to police right now.

You can download Tor at: www.torproject.org

Chapter 9:
A note about Antivirus software

I know, I know, you're still looking for that section about Antivirus software. Well, here it is.

I explicitly and deliberately didn't mention antiviruses throughout this text because I wanted to write a simple note about them, and since they are so popular, they deserve a separate chapter.

First of all, I'm sorry to inform you that antivirus softwares are no panacea, they are not a catch-all solution to all privacy problems going on in your PC. They are marketed as if they were, but, sorry again, they are not.

Second, common sense is your best bet in this case. Antivirus softwares are developed by corporations, they are usually costly (NOT FREE) and they are not open source.

When you install such software, trying to protect your files, your computer, which seems very intelligent, but is not, comes to believe that you trust your newly installed antivirus software. So, when you give access to your system to this antivirus you are actually giving it control over your computer, modifying your system, so everything that happens in it, you give it permission to do anything with it.

Let's get geeky here. A component of your antivirus is installed in your operating system kernel, hence each time you connect to the Internet, a document you write, a file you change, etc., it has to be reviewed and modified by your antivirus. That's a perfect world.

Now, in real life, when checking all the things you do, a bunch of milliseconds are spent doing it, if you are doing many tasks, the end result is that your PC will slow down A LOT.

The other thing is giving it so much control over your life, it is just asking for more problems. If you place all your trust in antivirus softwares, them, they may very well become one day a vector and prone to attacks. If someone, like one of those creepy cyberparasites, exploits an antivirus trust that you have given, they may do evil things to you, because not even your system may know about it. Like turning your camera on, your microphone, etc.

There is one exception though, and that is ClamAV, which is Free and it's also open source. The good thing about ClamAV is that its scanning is on-demand, not constantly, therefore not abusing of trust and also not slowing down the computer. The downside of ClamAV is that it's text-based (you will have to open a command screen and do geeky stuff that you may not be familiar with). However, there are friendlier versions without the command screen stuff. For Windows based computers, there is ClamWin. For Linux based systems, there is ClamTk.

You may download ClamAV here: clamav.net
You may download ClamWin here: clamwin.com
You may download ClamTk here: dave-theunsub.github.io/clamtk

Chapter 10:
A couple of final words

Well, look at you. You made it all the way to the end. I'm so proud of you. I know some parts of my book may have been extremely technical, and for that I beg excuses. But I couldn't go around trying to hide them. I had to tell them like it is without sugarcoating them. Sorry.

I hope you learned all the stuff that I threw at you. Some were easy to comprehend and others not so. But if you re-read a chapter that you may have not understood, you may grasp the basic concepts the second time around, and then you can put those same basic principles in practice.

Excuse if my language was irreverent, but you can't blame a 16 year-old, I think most of us talk that way.

As I told you in the beginning, I began writing this project at 13, so some parts may have a different tone of voice because they reflect my age then. It took me so long because I am involved in a variety of personal and school projects, so I had to apportion time during the night, during some weekends, and during very early hours in the morning, at the expense of my sleeping. But I think it was worth it.

I want to emphasize that I am not an expert nor I pretend to impersonate one, the material that I shared here with you has come from my personal experience, and from books, magazines and reports in the topic that I have read. I tried to give credit to all that I specifically mentioned. So, feel free to use my material, but do so at your own risk.

My next project? I'm in the final stage of a second Android App that is going to blow your mind. It's great, but I can't tell you more about it now. You'll have to wait until I publish it, which will be soon.

If you have any comment about this book or my Apps, please contact me through the Twitter account: @JonoApps

Thanks again, and may God always bless you and your family.

AND NOW,
A WORD
FROM MY SPONSOR
(my only one sponsor, sigh!)

Yes, that's me. I am my only sponsor.

You may follow this simple 3-step formula:

 If you haven't done so already, **PLEASE**,:

1) DOWNLOAD MY APP (It's **FREE**) at :

* jonathan-apps.com
* play.google.com (Search for it under: PrivatBrowse)

If you have a child/niece/nephew/grandchild/ neighbor/geek
buddy/a dog/a friendly alien,
and you haven't done so already, **PLEASE**:

2) BUY HIM/HER/IT A COPY OF THIS BOOK (It's **not** free,
sorry) at:

Amazon.com

And when you hear about my next App, **PLEASE**:

3) DOWNLOAD IT FROM THE SAME PLACES.

THANK YOU!